RAINBOW

A MIGRANT'S STORY

ARUN KUMAR SARKAR

BALBOA.
PRESS

A DIVISION OF HAY HOUSE

Balboa Press books may be ordered through booksellers or by contacting:

Balboa Press
A Division of Hay House
1663 Liberty Drive
Bloomington, IN 47403
www.balboapress.com.au
1 (877) 407-4847

Because of the dynamic nature of the Internet, any web addresses or
links contained in this book may have changed since publication and
may no longer be valid. The views expressed in this work are solely those
of the author and do not necessarily reflect the views of the publisher,
and the publisher hereby disclaims any responsibility for them.

The author of this book does not dispense medical advice or prescribe the use
of any technique as a form of treatment for physical, emotional, or medical
problems without the advice of a physician, either directly or indirectly. The
intent of the author is only to offer information of a general nature to help
you in your quest for emotional and spiritual well-being. In the event you use
any of the information in this book for yourself, which is your constitutional
right, the author and the publisher assume no responsibility for your actions.

Any people depicted in stock imagery provided by Thinkstock are
models, and such images are being used for illustrative purposes only.
Certain stock imagery © Thinkstock.

Printed in the United States of America.

ISBN: 978-1-4525-2561-7 (sc)
ISBN: 978-1-4525-2562-4 (e)

Balboa Press rev. date: 09/15/2014

CONTENTS

PREFACE

This is my story. I am an engineer currently living in Australia and this story follows my life path and how it came to be.

I had a rough ride during my childhood. The political upheaval in India during that time due to the riots as well as the Indo Pakistan war is something that no child should experience during their growing years.

After my graduation in Engineering in 1959 I got a job in Australia. But due to some unforeseen circumstances I had to go to Germany. I lived in Germany for almost 3 and half years. During the time that I lived in Germany (then West Germany) I travelled almost all over Europe. I came back to India in 1962, working in different cities like Delhi, Madras, Bangalore and Bombay.

In 1982 I migrated to Australia and at present I am living in Sydney, Australia. Like many other migrants I have had many ups and downs in my life, all of which are narrated here in this book.

I have two unforgettable memories that will never be erased from my mind. The first one was the journey from India to Italy by ship. This was my first time overseas and I will never forget the thrill of the adventure.

The second memory was my journey to the Alps. I have thoroughly enjoyed the drive along the river Rhine through the Black Forest and the sheer beauty of the land.

My wife has wholeheartedly supported me in this endeavour to retell my stories through this book.

I thank my wife and all those who inspired me to write.

I am also thankful to Mr. Swapan Banerjee, who is one of my friends, for helping me publish the book.

I am also thankful to Mrs Tilottama Sarkar for editing.

Arun Kumar Sarkar

This is a true story. The names mentioned in this book are not changed if not stated otherwise

1

MY CHILDHOOD

On 5 August 1934 I was born in a city called Siuri which is near the border of West Bengal and Bihar States on the eastern part of India It was a thunderous night. Because of this treacherous weather my relatives predicted that I would be a brave and strong man when I grow up. Now I can tell that they were all wrong. I grew up as a shy and a timid person.

In 1938 my father bought a piece of land in south Calcutta to build a house. This land is hardly a kilo metre from the famous Dhakuria Lake. The lake itself is about 1 and ½ Kilo meter long and at some places it is about 500 metre wide. It has got beautiful surroundings. At present there are 4 Rowing clubs. (Pictures 1 and 2 are of Dhakuria Lake). On both sides of this lake there was vast land which is now unrecognisable with buildings and streets that have slowly been built over the years.

The building that was our house was completed in 1939. It is a 3 storied building and on each floor my father built 6 bedrooms, two kitchens, two bathrooms and three balconies with a big hall in the centre. We were all eager to start our new life there and were looking forward to the future.

But then in 1939 World War II started.

I was then only 5 years old and did not have any idea about war. India was a British Colony at that time. I saw thousands of troops come to Calcutta and occupying houses and vacant lands. Hundreds of war tanks and trucks loaded with Anti Aircraft Guns arrived in Calcutta.

Dhakuria lake with its surroundings were occupied by the British and American soldiers who brought with them all sorts of war equipment. It became a major Army Base in the Eastern Region with its headquarters in Fort Williams which is about 8 km north east of the lake. The boundary of this Army Base was hardly 500 meters away from our house.

Calcutta was not safe to live in anymore. The Japanese army invaded from the east, conquered Burma and came to the door steps of India. In 1940, my father was transferred to Dacca and then to Moymonsing in East Bengal. (There was no East or West Bengal at that time. It was a unified Bengal. In 1947 when India became Independent, Bengal was divided into West Bengal and East Bengal) .

In 1942 the Quit India Movement started. It was a fight for India's Independence. It originated in Bengal and spread all over India. Indians were fighting the British who occupied

India for over 200 years. Many British and Indians were killed during this Quit India Movement. Mahatma Gandhi of course started the Non-violence movement much earlier but took momentum after 1942.

We lived in Moymonsing for three years. My schooling started there. When I was in Year 3 in school, my father was transferred back to Calcutta. It was 1943. I was then only 9 years old. I lost one year since I had to redo my Year 3 in school.

Picture 1 Dhakuria Lake West

Picture 2 Dhakuria Lake East

In 1943, my father became Chief Engineer of PWD (Public Works Dept.). He was the first Indian Chief Engineer in Bengal. Earlier this position was always held by British personnel and that had made my father's position very venerable. All those people who were in the Quit India movement thought my father was a supporter of the British Raj. This put my father's life at high risk and he opted for volunteer retirement.

The British in the meantime were very much anxious because of the war. The Japanese Army had come almost to the boundaries on the eastern side of India. The British arranged a meeting with leaders of the Quit India Movement including Mahatma Gandhi and assured them that if they withdrew the Freedom Movement and joined the British to fight against the Japanese Army then after the war India would be granted its Independence. After this meeting the "Quit India Movement" was called off and India started preparing for its Independence by joining hands with the British against the Japanese.

The World War II was over in 1945 and India got its Independence on 15th of August 1947. But the independence of India did not come on a golden platter.

The struggle for independence had started sometime in 19th century, around the year 1850. In the beginning many people who fought for the independence were killed. Those who were a part of the struggle for independence were arrested and many of them were sentenced to death and some were jailed in the Andaman Islands. A Bastille like jail was constructed on Port Blair in the Andamans to house hundreds of such freedom fighters and convicts who were never set free and were systematically hanged to death. Only very few freedom fighters escaped the death sentence.

Picture 3 Cellular Jail in Port Blair, Andaman Islands

Picture 4 Torture inside the Cellular Jail

Picture 5 Inside the Cellular Jail Compound

Those freedom fighters and the convicts who were sent to Cellular Jail in Port Blair, Andaman, were known as prisoners sentenced to "Kala Pani". The term 'Kala Pani' became synonymous with the transportation to the penal settlements beyond the sea. According to some expression "Kala Pani" has been used with reference to the Sanskrit word 'Kal' which means 'Time of Death'. The term 'Kala Pani', therefore, meant "Water of Death" or "A Place of Death" from where no one could return. For those who were sent to Andaman, Kala Pani virtually meant cruel and inhuman treatment for the rest of their life. It was considered worse than the Death Penalty.

After the war there was tremendous shortage of food. The poorest of the poor started dying of starvation. It happened not just in Bengal but all over India. I have seen dead bodies lying on the footpath. The ravages of the war was too painful for me to forget as it happened during a very tender age.

Then came the communal riot, Hindus versus Muslims that started in 1946. It all started because Mr. Jinna wanted to be the first Prime Minister of India, and Mr Nehru vehemently opposed saying that India's majority population was Hindu and therefore he should be the first Prime Minister of India. In response Mr. Jinna then declared to have a separate state for Muslims. Thus started a communal riot. Thousands of Hindus and Muslims were killed by each other. Mahatma Gandhi went to Noakhali (a city in East Bengal) and started a hunger strike and pledged that he would continue fasting until the riot was stopped. But both the parties were adamant and asked Mr. Gandhi whether the idea of dividing India was acceptable to him because that was the only way to stop the riot. To avoid the killings of Hindus and Muslims Mr. Gandhi ultimately and reluctantly agreed to the proposal. So ultimately India was divided in August 14, 1945 and Pakistan was born.

During the riot, one day, I was on the 3rd floor balcony of our house when I saw a Muslim man beaten to death by a gang of Hindus. He was beaten on the head mercilessly by hockey sticks. He was just a hawker selling fruits. I did not really understand what was achieved by killing an innocent poor man. It was so deplorable and shocking. I was then 12 years of age and now I m 80 and that scene still haunts me and I still do not understand.

This was my childhood.

2

DAWN OF MY CAREER

Slowly I got used to the political upheaval and carried on with my studies. I graduated (Bachelor of Science) from Calcutta University. While studying B.Sc, I joined National Cadet Corp (NCC) in their Air Wings Division and took this course as my fourth subject in B.Sc. I did fairly well as an Air Wings Cadet. During the final year I was promoted to the rank of Warrant Officer. At that time the Chief of the Air Staff was Air Vice Marshal Subrata Mukherje. He visited our Air Wings Hanger where he gave us a lecture on the future of the Air force in India. There I personally expressed my strong desire to join the Air Force. (See Picture 6).

Picture 6 Talking to Air Vice Marshall Subrata Mukherjee

I appeared for the selection to join the Air Force. Though selected but due to some family reasons I did not join the Air force. I should have taken this decision before I applied for the selection.

I had changed my choice of career and wanted to be an engineer. I got admitted in an Engineering College in Madras in the faculty of Electronics and studied there staying in College Hostel. The Institute of Technology is about 18 KM south of the city of Madras. The hostels were within the walking distance from the Institute buildings.

Madras is a very hot and humid city. We used to say that Madras has got three seasons; they are Hot, Hotter and Hottest. It is so very humid during summer that sometimes we had to take warm water baths to wash the body salt that settles on the skin from the sweat.

It was a hot and humid summer day in July 1959. I was returning back to my hostel from the classroom. On the way back to the hostel I met one of my friends who told me that the Postman was waiting for me to deliver a registered letter. I hurried to my hostel, met the Postman and took delivery of the registered letter. It was a letter from Philips Australia, Melbourne. I remembered I applied for a job when I was in the final semester in the Engineering College. I thought I would never get any reply from them. I opened the letter. I was really surprised and filled with joy when I read the letter. A job was offered to me in their TV factory subject to my getting the Degree in Electronics Engineering and getting the entry permit to Australia. I was offered 1100 Pounds per year to start with, which was not a bad amount in those days (1959). I had always wanted to go to Australia. I had read so many things about this country, about the people, the convicts and of course about the natural beauty of the land.

The final Exams finished. I packed my belongings and came to my hometown Calcutta. In due course the Exam results were released and I passed securing good marks in almost all the subjects. I had had ranked first in the Electro Magnetic Theory paper. My father had passed away the previous year. My mother was wondering why I was not trying to get a job instead of wandering around. I then disclosed to her that I had already got a good job in Australia and I would be going there soon. I told her that the job was in Philips Company in Melbourne, Australia. Mother did not like the idea of my going to Australia.

She asked, "Why you want to go to Australia, why not to Germany? Your younger brother is in Germany studying Engineering there. If you go there then you two can stay together and help each other. You will also not feel lonely and I will get some peace of mind."

I knew the reason why she did not like me to go to Australia. At that time Australia was known as a land of convicts, farmers and cultivators.

However, without wasting any more time, I booked my passage to Australia by ship. It was a fully Air-conditioned Motor Ship and had a capacity of, as far as I can remember, 1500 passengers. It was one of the ships of an Italian shipping liner. The ship sailed from Genoa in Italy to Sydney touching the port of Cochin in India. I also applied to the Australian Consulate for the entry permit to Australia. In those days Indians were never required to apply for entry permit or visa to go to the U.K. most probably because both are members of the Commonwealth countries and Indians are considered as British subject. Since Australia is also a Commonwealth country, I thought most stupidly that to apply for the Entry Permit to Australia was just a formality. But I got a shock later just 15 days before the departure date of my ship from Cochin. I received a letter from the Australian Consulate that my application for the Entry Permit was not successful. But if I wanted to go to Australia for further study then my application for entry to Australia would be re-considered and most probably I would get one. I went to the Australian

Consulate office for further clarification. The officer in the Consulate office was reluctant to give me any details. When I explained that I had already booked the passage and made full payment, which I believe, I should not have done, he then in a very modest way explained the White Australia Policy to me. I immediately protested naively saying that I was not a black person, rather brown.

But I should have known that brown is not white either.

I then contacted the Shipping Company and applied for the refund of money I paid for the passage from Cochin to Sydney stating the reason for the cancellation of my trip to Australia. Within a short time I received a reply from them advising me that it would not be possible to refund the money because the ship had sailed out of Italy with a vacant berth for me. However, since the cancellation was due to no fault of mine, they would provide me with a free ticket to Genoa from Cochin in the same ship returning from Sydney. I immediately agreed to this offer.

This is how I wanted to go to Australia but found myself in Europe instead.

3

TO INDIAN HARBOUR, COCHIN, ON MY JOURNEY TO EUROPE

I got the ticket to go to Europe all right, but where in Europe do I go? An idea came in my mind. I immediately wrote to my younger brother who was studying in the then West Germany explaining all that had happened in connection with my trip to Australia. I wrote, "Now I have a ticket to Genoa. The ship is likely to anchor at Cochin sometime in mid September 1959. Could you please arrange a job for me there and send me an appointment letter as quickly as possible so that I can obtain a Visa for West Germany before the ship sails away from India." And he did. He arranged a job for me in a company where he worked for some time during vacations.

I got everything ready for the journey. A journey to a country where everything is different to what I was accustomed to. The climate is different, the customs are different, the food is different, and the language is different. I was 23 years old and scared of the unknown. This was the first time I felt helpless. I never knew what 'helpless' felt like. Since everything had been arranged and finalised there was no going back. I felt as if I was sailing on a 'river of no return'. I was on my way and I had to go.

I received a letter from the shipping agent advising me that I should report at Cochin dockyard on 17th of September 1959.

I boarded the train in Calcutta on 15 September so as to reach Cochin on 17th morning. I had to travel to Madras from Calcutta then catch another train at Madras to go to Cochin. But as unfortunate as I am, the Calcutta-Madras train was late by 4 hours due to some minor accident of another train ahead of us. I missed the Madras-Cochin Express train. I could not take the next day's train from Madras, as I would miss the ship.

There were few more passengers like me who were going to Cochin to board the ship. We were altogether nine people. So the only alternative was to fly from Madras to Cochin. We had to hire nine taxis to carry our luggage and us to the Indian Airlines Office in the city. There were no tickets available on the direct flight to Cochin. However, they could issue tickets in their hopping flight, which would stop at four Airports on the way. This was a Focker Friendship aeroplane. In those days passengers could check-in in the Airlines office in the city instead of at the airport. While checking in, the trouble started again. Only 20 Kg of luggage was allowed per person. Most of us were carrying about 60 Kg luggages, and some of us even had Steel Trunks. The officer told us that no way he could allow us to carry that amount of luggage even if we pay for the excess luggage. This was a small plane and the plane would be over loaded. We then explained to him why we were carrying so much of luggage. We showed our ship boarding tickets. We could not fly next day because the ship would not wait for us. The officer then talked to the Manager who then had a telephone conversation with some higher authority. The Manager then came to us with a big smiling face, which meant that he definitely had some good news for us.

"Yes", he said, "you all can go with your luggage; we are off loading some of our cargo to accommodate you people. Wish you all the best and a very enjoyable journey to Europe".

After having our Boarding Pass issued, we rushed to the airport. At last we were on our way to Cochin to catch the ship. We landed safely at Cochin though the journey was quite bumpy. We collected our luggage and proceeded to the harbour in a convoy of taxis. When we reached the destination it was almost dark. The sun had already set and the western sky was little reddish.

The ship was there in front of us waiting for the passengers to board. In front of the jetty there was the Marine Club. The clubhouse had an architectural beauty. It had quite a big restaurant, which could be seen from outside through the big glass windows and a huge open and nicely decorated balcony as a dining area. After this hectic and tiresome journey from Calcutta I did not feel like having any food at that time. In the meantime I had developed a friendship with my fellow travellers. Opposite to the Clubhouse there were temporary check-in counters and the departure lounge, which was a makeshift arrangement. There was a small crowd at the front of a counter. I approached the counter and managed to talk to the officer. On inquiring I was told that they would start issuing the boarding passes only at 12 O'clock night. It was, as far as I can remember, about 6 O'clock in the evening. So we would have to wait for at least 6 more hours to get into the immigration area. The whole area was quite crowded.

The transit passengers, who were on their way to Europe from Australia, were allowed to disembark the ship and entertain themselves in the Marine Clubhouse. There was about 500 to 600-transit passengers, most of them were European. Some of them were inside the Clubhouse and gossiping and few were outside on the balcony and on the open green lawn. Most of them including the ladies were drinking. Gents were happy with the beer as could be easily guessed from their shouting and laughing. It was too early for dinner and definitely for us Indians who never had dinner earlier than 9:00 pm. I looked at my watch. It was around 6.30PM. I lazily walked around then entered the Clubhouse. I met all the five friends again inside the Clubhouse and occupied a large table. The eldest of us whose name was Mr.Tapan Mukherjee, whom we called Tapanda later on (Indian way rather Bengali way of respecting elder person by adding 'da' after the name and placing him on the level of elder brother), bought six big bottles of beer for all of us. I had never drunk any alcohol previously. I was little bit hesitant to drink beer but Tapanda insisted and said that since I was going to Germany I better start drinking beer. In Germany that was the only thing I would be able to drink because tap water was no good there. Tapanda had been living in UK for the last 15 to 16 years. He came to India on holidays to meet his relatives. He was a confirmed bachelor. So I learnt to drink beer and frankly I liked the taste, though I never developed into a regular beer drinker.

Slowly people started coming in and gathered in front of the check-in counter and on the lawn in front of the clubhouse. It was then around 8 O'clock and we decided to have some food and take some rest. It would be definitely mid-night before we could board the ship and take a nap. We had our food and came out of the club restaurant at about 9 PM. There were hundreds of passengers with their entire luggage waiting on the lawn for check-in.

What surprised me was the number of Sikh families going to Europe. Was there any religious festival going to be held in Europe? There were at least 200 Sikh families. That is with wives and the children there would be around 800 Sikh persons. Most of the Sikh men folks there looked alike. They all had similar colour turban, similar beard and almost similar clothing. It was almost difficult to recognise one from the other. We six started discussing this and concluded that they were definitely going to Europe to attend some religious festival and most probably in the U.K. We became inquisitive and started talking to them. They did not know the English language at all. They were speaking in Punjabi but it seemed to be a dialect of the Punjabi language, which was generally spoken in the interior villages. What we understood was that they were going to London. They were not going there to attend any religious festival. They were going to London to work and for the time being they would stay with their respective relatives or friends.

I started wondering what job could they do, since they could not even speak the language of the land, leave aside any experience they could use there? But any way that was their business and I had too much to worry about myself.

One of us then raised a question on how could they get the passports and visa for U.K? Tapanda, who was more experienced in overseas travelling matters than any of us informed us that Indians did not require any Visa to go to U.K. (This was in 1959). However how they managed to get the passports was a big question mark. And it was answered later on.

4

JOURNEY TO EUROPE

It was 12.30 AM when the check-in started. We all checked in one by one through ten different counters. The trouble started again at the immigration counters. All the Sikh passengers, 800 of them, were called to one side and about fifteen to twenty immigration officers started discussing something with them. Another group of officers were whispering. It was some serious matter, obvious from their body language.

One of the officers had a few passports in his hand, which he was showing to his colleagues. I could guess from their expression that the matter was serious. However, those who had their passports checked and stamped were requested to proceed to the ship. So ultimately at around 3 O'clock morning we six boarded the ship and went to our respective berths. Fortunately we six were given berths in the same six-berth cabin. We all had economy class tickets. We were so tired that all of us went straight to bed except Tapanda. He said he would like to go to the upper deck for fresh air. He did not want to sleep then because only after an hour or so it would in any case be morning.

I think I just slept may be for a few minutes when some one vigorously shook me and woke me up. I opened my eyes and saw Tapanda standing in front of me and other four friends were hurriedly dressing up.

I asked Tapanda with my eyes wide open from surprise "What has happened? Is something wrong?"

He said "I will tell you all about it later, but first change quickly and come with us, be quick."

So we went hurriedly to the lower deck of the ship which was meant for the economy class ticket holders. The sight that met my eyes was worse than any refugee camp I had ever seen in my life (in pictures during the war). It was a pretty big deck but fully crowded. The luggage was stacked at one side of the deck. There were five tables at the cabin side of the deck, which were occupied by the officers of the ship. The Captain of the ship with a few other officers was discussing something when we reached there. Seeing us the Captain gave a big sigh of relief. He immediately came to us and shook hands with Tapanda. He told the Captain that he should not worry at all and we would sort out the entire problem. He then introduced us to the captain. He represented us six like a leader.

I said out loud "What was the problem? Why do we need to sort out their issues? We are not officers of the ship".

Then the Captain said to us that without our help he would not be able to provide any services to those passengers (pointing his hand towards the crowd on the deck).

He said, "They do not speak English. There are more than one, may be five, people by the same name. Most of them look alike. You will have to help us assist them".

Then he instructed the other officers, who were on duty there, to wait for half an hour. He then took us to his sitting room, which was attached to his cabin. He said that the voyage from Cochin to Genoa was for approximately 3 weeks. If we agreed to work for him then he would give us accommodation in the first class cabin and all the other facilities that go with it. He could not pay us cash but the offer he made was within his power. We agreed and celebrated our upgrade to first class hurriedly with champagne, which the Captain very gladly offered.

We came down to the lower deck to start the work. At first we thought it was an easy task, but it wasn't. The people were very simple and honest. I think they came from interior villages and did not really have any idea of life outside a village. They were simple and pure in all respects. That was the reason, which we found later on, how they were so easily cheated by some crook from Bombay.

Our first duty was to identify each person and his luggage. We had a bunch of passports with us. We opened one passport and called out the name, Abtar Singh. Five Abtar Singhs came in front of us. We then found 5 passports with the same name. They also looked almost alike. We asked them to take their own passport and each one of them took one. Then they were allowed to take their wives' and children's passports.

I asked Tapanda "Are you sure they have taken their own passports and their own wives and children".

He said "Why bother, we will never be able to find that. At least they got back their passports".

Then they were asked to identify their luggage. And they did. But how they did it was a mystery. All their belongings did look alike. I asked the same question to Tapanda. He answered the same thing "Why bother, we will never be able to find that. At least let them be happy that they have got back their belongings".

Then we distributed the Cabin Cards that showed the cabin numbers and the berth numbers. One of us then guided them to their cabins. We told them that breakfast would be served in the Dining Hall at 7 AM. It was already 4 :00 am. Then we called out the next name, Jaginder Singh. Seven Jaginder Singhs came in front of us. And the same drama was re-enacted. I asked the same question. Tapanda gave the same answer.

"Why bother …".

It took us two and half hours to complete the formalities. When we finished it was 6.30 AM. The sky had lightened. We had not slept for two nights. It was very difficult to keep our eyes open when a cool breeze started blowing through the open deck of the ship. We never realised that the next shock was just waiting for us round the corner.

We could hear a noise that was gradually growing louder. We all looked at Tapanda.

I said, "What is it now?"

We realised that the noise was coming from the Dining Hall . We hurried towards the hall. We saw some of the Punjabis knocking at the entrance door to the hall.

We asked them "What's the matter?"

One of them replied "You said that breakfast would be served at 7 in the morning. It is already 7.15 and they have not yet opened the door."

We looked at our watch. It was then 6.45 AM. Their watches showed 7.15 AM. We then realised what had happened. We told them that they were to turn back their watches by half an hour and that it was announced the day before over the intercom. This was required because we were going towards the west. But this need not be half an hour every day. This might vary day to day and they should listen to the announcement that would be made every day at 10 O'clock night. By the time things were settled, it was 7 AM and the entrance door of the dining hall was opened. We could guess they were really hungry and felt for them as they rushed into the hall.

Again we had a job on our hands to explain the norms of the dining hall to almost 400 people leaving aside the children. So after about an hour when things settled down, we went to the upper deck in the 1st class Dining Room for our break fast. Seeing us entering the dining room the Captain himself came forward to welcome us. He took us to a table at the end of the room and thanked us for all saying his staff could not have done the job as we did and he was very grateful for our help.

We explained that these people are basically very good and very simple by nature with almost no exposure to the outside world.

We then requested the Captain whether it would be possible to provide them with Indian style food. He said he had already instructed the same but he expressed his doubt whether his staff would be able to prepare the Indian food properly.

We had just finished our breakfast and were having a hot cup of coffee and a cigarette. The Captain was enjoying his Pipe as usual. At that time whilst we were enjoying the lovely morning the whistle blew for us again. A second or a third Officer came to our table to report the Captain. We could guess from his face that the matter was very serious. The gist of the situation was like this:

The Lower three decks or floors were for the economy class. Each floor, so far as I could remember, had ten toilet/shower bays, and each bay again had ten toilets and ten showers. About 50% of those were for the ladies and remaining was for the men. They were identified by signboards like "Ladies" and "Men" both in English and Italian Language. But those passengers neither could read English nor Italian. So, you could imagine what had happened. We were really feeling helpless at that time.

To manage so many passengers and guide them properly was a heck of a job. We had to. We had to justify the good treatment we received from the Captain in a proper way. Tapanda brought a bunch of white cardboard papers and few felt pens. We caught hold of a person who could write in Punjabi language. Pictures were also drawn on the card board paper. So new signboards were made and installed at proper places. We six were posted at different places at different times. They were quite intelligent people. It took only two days, I think, to bring everything under control. However it took little longer time to convince them about adjusting the watches regularly every night.

Though it was September, it was getting hotter day by day as we were approaching the Red Sea. The air was warm and I preferred to spend the evening on the open deck. One evening when I was wandering on the deck alone I met a group of four people who were travelling from India. They introduced themselves and said they were travelling in the economy class. I could not recognise their faces. When I told that, they said, "Yes naturally, we had been to the hair dresser. We have had our hair cut and shaved. We don't want to wear turbans any more".

It made me sad that they felt they had to cut their hair to fit in. I was also worried for them about the border checks since they were unrecognisable without the turbans. I exclaimed and said, "You should not have done this. Now you may have trouble with the immigration officers. There will hardly be any resemblance between your passport photos and you."

Later on I told this to Tapanda at the dining table. He said, "It is not the pass port photos; it is the passport itself, which will give them trouble. I had a little chat with the Captain this afternoon. He is very worried. The thing is that many passengers, mostly those who came from the interior villages of Punjab have forged passports. Of course the authority is not very sure about it at this time. The Captain did not tell anything further and preferred to wait till he receives further information from Genoa."

Next few days passed without any major incident.

I really enjoyed the final days of sea voyage. During the day, though it was very hot under the sun, one could enjoy the beautiful fresh cool sea breeze if one stood in the shade. Sometimes the ocean was blue and sometimes it was little greenish. I have never seen such clear real blue skies. I really enjoyed lying on the deck chair and watching the night sky and gazing at the countless stars. Slowly I used to fall asleep on the deck chair as cool breezes blew across the ocean.

Sometimes I used to feel lonely. At night I used to go to the lower deck and walk along the railing from Stern to Bow. Even at night at 11 or 12 O'clock many passengers would just relax by sitting on the deck chairs or on the deck itself. They were either couples or lone star watchers. One day when I was taking my last round of walk on the deck and was at the Stern end I saw a young man sobbing. He was quite young. He was sitting on the deck with his head down resting on his knees. I sat behind him and asked whether he was OK? He kept silent for some time and then asked me "Do all parents sacrifice everything for the sake of their children?" "Why are you asking this?" I asked.

"No", he said. "It just came across my mind".

I said, "No it cannot just come across your mind. Tell me what it is. You will feel much lighter and better if you tell me" I said.

Then he said, "You see, I wanted to study Engineering. I am a good student and obtained very good marks in the exams. But let me say, an Engineering Institute has got 150 seats and there are 200 applicants for admission who are very good students. The Institute takes only 150 students - that does not mean that those remaining 50 applicants are no good. I am one of those applicants who were unsuccessful. Now my father is spending all his savings he had to send me abroad to study Engineering. Are all parents like this?"

I answered "Yes, most of the parents are like this. Don't get depressed and keep all whatever you said in your mind. After you have finished your study you go home and serve your parents and your country."

I got up and slowly walked towards our cabin feeling nostalgic. I was already homesick.

After we entered the Suez Canal, a group of passengers alighted on small boats and went to the shore. They took the conducted tour of Egypt to see Cairo and the Pyramids. They would join us again at Cairo. I was very much tempted to take that conducted tour, but due to financial constraints I had to restrain myself. I consoled myself by thinking that later on I would get enough time to visit Cairo and the Pyramids. The ship was moving very slowly through the Canal. Suddenly we were surrounded by floating markets. Various items from souvenirs to utilities were for sale. You had to bargain a lot if you wanted to buy something from them.

So ultimately we came to the end of the Suez Canal and after a while those passengers who went in the tour joined us. On our way to Genoa we halted at Sicily for about six hours and at Naples for about 12 hours. Like many passengers I also got down at Sicily. We had only four hours to wander around the town. It was a nice and very clean city.

When our ship anchored at Naples we six decided to get down and go to the city to enjoy the evening. It was about 5 O'clock in the afternoon and we were all dressed up for the evening. When Tapanda and the four others passed through the immigration desk on the ship, I realised that I had to en-cash some traveller's cheques. I told them to proceed and I would join them in a few minutes. It took only five minutes or so to en-cash the cheques and cross the immigration desk. They were about half a kilometre away and I was hurrying to catch them. When I was about 100 metres behind them a group of four young men, about my age, approached me and asked what the time was like. I raised my wrist to see the watch when one of them gave me a big blow on my face. Another person grabbed my wrist. A third person lifted my wallet from my back pocket. I could not do anything against those thugs except shouting loudly to attract my friend's attention. When I got up from the ground, I saw blood oozing out through my nose. They came running towards me, but by that time those thugs fled away. My wristwatch had vanished, my wallet gone but I felt my passport was still there in the inside breast pocket of my jacket. There was not much money in the wallet, but I felt very upset about the wristwatch. It was a costly watch presented by my elder brother before I left for Europe. I felt so bad that I wanted to come back to the ship, but my friends insisted that I went with them to enjoy the evening. During the entire evening I was remembering the brutal attack on me and it was haunting me like nightmare. I heard about such muggings that happen in Italy, especially in the southern part of Italy. Similar things happened again after four years when I was coming back to India. But it did not happen to me physically that time. When my return to India was settled, I sent my entire luggage to India by ship. In Genoa my luggage was broken into and some items were stolen. This part of my story comes later but that was the second time I felt violated.

After returning to the ship I reported the incident to the Captain. He felt bad about it because the ship was an Italian Liner and all crews including the Captain were Italian. I however said that it was not only in Italy, we could find thugs everywhere in this world.

We sailed out from Naples at night for Genoa. In the morning at around 10 O'clock next day we reached Genoa. I got up early in the morning and packed everything I had. We all six went together to the dining room for our last breakfast on the ship. When we entered the room we saw the Captain. He asked us to take seat at his table. He thanked us once again for all the work we did for the passengers. He asked us whether we enjoyed our voyage and then looked at me with a meaningful smile. We of course said that the voyage was wonderful. He then presented each of us a gift packet. We opened our packets and were surprised and delighted to find a gold watch in every packet. He then most humbly said to us that he would be very happy if we accept this small gift from him. And we were of course happy to make him happy.

Then he broke the unsavoury news. He said that the Indian Embassy Officers and the Italian Immigration Officers had come aboard. They had suspected some foul play regarding the passports of the passengers who boarded the ship at Cochin. The Captain told those officers about us and we would help them if needed. It took about four hours to clear all the passengers with Indian passports. About 180 Sikh passengers were asked not to leave the ship and their passports were seized. We then talked to them to find out what had happened. They wanted to go to England to stay with their relatives and also do work there to earn their livelihood. One of them approached a company in Bombay who would arrange to get passports for them. This was how some non-scrupulous businessman from Bombay cheated these honest and simple people. It was not possible to help them in any way. These passengers would be sent back to India by the same ship. Who would pay for their passage? It was a question to be resolved by the Shipping Liner and the Embassy of India. Young and carefree as I was, as far as I was concerned, I was free to land in Italy and proceed further to Germany.

I said adieu to my friends at the immigration counter and proceeded towards the gate. Suddenly I heard someone call me by my nickname. Who in Genoa could possibly know my nickname? I turned around and saw my elder brother. He was Chief Engineer of an Indian Cargo Liner. He got the information from my mother about my approximate date of arrival at Genoa and the name of the ship. He kept a track of the movement of the ship and there he was. He took me to his ship and I spent 3 days there. I was overjoyed and for the first time in days completely relaxed to see a familiar face.

5

MY HARDEST DAYS IN GERMANY

After spending three days with my brother on his ship I boarded a train for Aachen in Germany. Before I boarded the train I sent a telegram to my younger brother with my arrival details. Next morning I arrived in Aachen. My younger brother, Barun was at the station to receive me along with few of his friends. Aachen is in the northwest of Germany. It was the first week of October and very cold at that time of the year. We drove to the hostel where Barun was staying.

Most of the people in Aachen were students of the Aachen Technical College. They were mostly from foreign countries. You could hardly see a German in Aachen. I stayed there with my brother for few days, and then went to Frankfurt in West Germany. My brother arranged a job for me in a communication maintenance firm in Frankfurt.

It was a small company run by a family. The owner was the Director and his wife was the secretary. I was the only engineer appointed and there were two supervisors. Most of the other people working there were labourers. Only the owner and his wife could speak tolerably good English. The remaining employees spoke only German. I could not speak German because I didn't get time to do so before I left India for Germany. It was not an enviable situation. My boss gave me a fortnight's time to learn the language, at least to the extent, that I could carry on my work with the other employees. To learn a new language to the level that I could converse with others was practically impossible. So the consequence was obvious. Though my boss wanted an engineer very badly but I was naturally useless and I had to leave the company after two weeks. During the 50s in Germany there was a tremendous shortage of engineers and other professionals. This was an after war effect. However my employer turned out to be a very kind person and a perfect gentleman. He arranged a job for me in a steel rod manufacturing company in Hagen. He gave me a farewell dinner at his residence. Next day he and his wife came to the Railway Station to see me off.

Hagen is an industrial town with a few thousand people and not far from Cologne and Bonn. The name of the company was Poupliar Stahl Werk. After my arrival I directly went to the factory and introduced myself. They knew about my coming to Hagen. They had arranged my stay with a German family as a paying guest. I was asked to commence my work from the next day. In the meantime they would arrange my work permit and I should report to the police about my stay in Hagen. That was the law of the country. I think this law is still in force. So I went to the Police Station near my residence where my stay was arranged. I registered my arrival by giving all the details including the address of my new residence. Registration with my nil knowledge of German and their broken English was a tough job. I spoke broken German with terrible pronunciation and the form to be filled in was in German language. Anyway, after I had completed the formalities with the police, I slowly walked down the street and came to my new home. It was not far from the Police Station. An elderly woman opened the door. I greeted her and somehow introduced myself. She was Frau Hoffman, the landlady. She already knew about my coming there and had made all the arrangements. She guided me to a room where I would stay. It was a medium sized room furnished with a bed, bedside table, a small dressing table, a table and a chair. The room had two windows overlooking a beautiful garden which happened to be the front garden. The leaves of the trees had already started falling since it was autumn. Winter was approaching and the temperature had dropped to around 12 degree C. The room was very comfortably warm since the house was centrally heated. I looked around the room and then told her that everything was very satisfactory. Then she guided me to the sitting room. It was a well-decorated cosy room with a big TV set at one corner. She started talking to me in German Language.

I replied in English "I am sorry, I do not speak German".

Most probably she understood because next moment she moved her hand towards her mouth and then put her hand on her belly and then asked me "Ya?"

By that time I had learnt a few German words. Immediately I said "Ya, bitte" because I was really feeling hungry.

It was almost 2 O'clock in the afternoon. She then got up and walked towards the kitchen and I went to my room to unpack my suitcases. After about half an hour or so she came back with a tray in her hand. She brought some German bread slices, slices of cold meat and various types of cheese and a pot of German coffee. It was a treat. I was so hungry I ate almost everything then settled with a cup of coffee and a cigarette. I was feeling tired. I lied down on the bed and tried to sleep. It was evening when I got up and went to the bathroom to wash my face. I saw Herr Hoffman while coming back to my room. I did not talk to him because of the language but we both raised our hands to greet each other. After a while I was summoned to the sitting room. The whole family Hoffman was there. After completing the shake hand round I settled on a couch. They had three children, one son and two daughters. The son was the eldest one and his name was Gerhard and about 28 years of age. The eldest daughter, Dolly, was about 19 and the younger one, Tina, was about 17 years old and the naughtiest.

It was a great relief to know that Herr Hoffman could speak English to some extent and Gerhard was quite good at English. Dolly and Tina were learning English at school. Frau Hoffman told something to her husband and they discussed something, which I could not understand. Then Herr Hoffman said, "Sorry, my wife doesn't speak English. You see, we have got another paying guest here. He pays

50 DMarks per fortnight in advance for the room, which includes linen washing and changing and a pot of Coffee or tea in the morning, and again in the evening. And one time deposit of 50 DMarks. I think it will be alright for you."

I said, " Yes, it is alright for me".

I had with me only about 150 Marks. I paid 100 Marks to him and said, "Thank you very much for allowing me to stay here."

50 DMarks per week for a room with bed and tea/coffee was not a small amount in those days. I was very much worried to realise that I would have to pull on with remaining 50 DMarks for the next whole week before I could get some money. Frau Hoffman again said something to her husband. Then Herr Hoffman looked at me and said, "We will be very happy if you could join us for the dinner".

I gladly accepted the invitation. With 50 DMarks in the pocket I could not say 'no'. Both Dolly and Tina were smiling all along during our conversation. May be because we were talking only in English and that was quite funny for them.

So we sat for the dinner. I asked them who was the other paying guest living here. What was his name and when would he come back. Gerhard replied, "He is your country man. He is also from Calcutta like you. His name is Khokon. Normally he comes back at around 10 O'clock night but sometimes he comes back early. He stays next to your room."

Khokon was obviously the nickname. I was very happy to know that someone was there with whom I could make friendship. Of course the family Hoffman was there for help if needed be. I enjoyed the hot dinner. It was the first time in my life that I ate beef. I had never eaten beef before on religious grounds. My hunger however got the better of me. After all German cows are not religious cows – are they?. This was the consolation I gave to myself. Anyway "When you are in Rome, do as Romans do".

After dinner we all went to the sitting room and the TV was switched on. The two daughters were cutting jokes with me partly in English and partly in German. Gerhard was discussing something with his mother. Herr Hoffman asked me, "Arun, have you brought anything for the breakfast tomorrow."

I said, "No, I will buy something tomorrow on my way to work."

He said, "You will not find any shop open at those hours in the morning. My wife will prepare some sandwiches for you." Then he laughingly added "Only for tomorrow."

I didn't say anything, just smiled as my consent. It was already 9 o'clock and I wanted to go back to my room to complete unpacking my suitcases. I said good night to them and thanked them for the nice dinner.

When I just finished my unpacking Khokon dropped in. He introduced himself and said that he was also working in the same factory 'Poupliar Stahl Werk'. He already heard from the firm about my joining and it was he who fixed up my stay here with the Hoffman family. I thanked him for the trouble he had taken for me.

I said, "So, we will go to the factory tomorrow at 6 O'clock morning. The factory is not far off from this place and is hardly a 5 minute walk".

He said, "Yes, you are right. Have you got proper clothes? Because it is very cold in the morning and you will have to wear warm clothes. Have you got thick woollen overcoat?"

No, I didn't have that. I had two woollen suits, two not-so-good pullovers, few shirts and underwear's. I opened the wardrobe and showed him all what I had.

He said, "No Arun, this is not sufficient. You will definitely catch a cold if not pneumonia. I can lend you a sweater and a thick good pullover for the time being. Our work will be over by 4 O'clock. There is a good clothes store nearby which remains open till 6 O'clock. I will take you there. You must buy a few things by tomorrow."

I asked him how much would that cost me?

He said, "One good overcoat will cost say 120 DMarks, Two good pullovers will cost another say 60 DMarks and two long woollen under wears will cost another 20 DMarks. So altogether it will cost you around 200 DMarks".

I said, "Forget it. I cannot buy all that stuff".

"Why?", he enquired.

I said I had only 50 DMarks in my pocket and I required that money for my food for the whole of next week.

He kept quiet for some time then said, "You cannot go out like that in summer clothing. You must have proper outfit. Do one thing, if you don't mind. I will give you 200 DMarks on loan just like that, no interest. Please do not protest. Return the money when you can. There is no hurry".

I nodded and said OK feeling a bit embarrassed though grateful. While leaving my room he asked what the time was. I told him that I didn't have watch and then narrated the whole story about what happened to me in Naples. Then he laughingly asked me whether I had an Alarm clock to wake me up in the morning.

I said, "Yes, I have one, I brought it from India".

I set the Alarm clock at 5 O'clock morning and went to bed. I slept like a dead man. At 5 O'clock I got up from the bed, brushed my teeth, washed my face and got ready for work. When I had changed and was ready Dolly knocked and entered with a pot of coffee and some sandwiches. I thanked her for bringing the breakfast.. As soon as breakfast was over Khokon entered the room and asked whether I was ready. The two of us then rushed out of the house.

It took hardly 5 minutes to reach the factory. Khokon showed me the way to the Personnel Department and went inside the factory. I did not know where exactly he used to work. However, I went to the Personnel Department and asked what I should do next. The lady at the desk gave me the Work Permit issued by the German Government. She then told me the name of the department where I would be working and gave me directions on how to go there. She also asked me to see the person in the security office at the exit gate before I left the factory premises in the afternoon.

While going to the work place I saw and read the Work Permit. Blood rushed to my head from sheer anger. This was not the job I had negotiated and expected.

Under the column Qualification it was written B.Sc. B.E. (Dipl. Ing.) (The Diploma in Engineering in Germany is Equivalent to Bachelor of Engineering Degree. In some places it is even considered as equivalent to Masters of Engineering Degree.) So this was alright. But under the job designation it said "Floor Sweeper". A graduate Engineer has to work as a Sweeper. That made me terribly sick. But my hands were tied. I didn't know the language of the land. I was almost on the verge of weeping. Somehow I reached the section where I was supposed to work. The foreman came forward and shook my hand. I gave him the work permit. He saw it and then gave it back to me. I could guess his age about 35 years old. I was then just 23 years old. He looked at me from my head to toe and then looked at my face again.

He asked me in clear English language "You want to work here as a floor sweeper?"

I asked, "Do I have any other choice? I cannot speak German Language."

I came to know later on that his father was British and mother was German. They were married before the war. His English was pretty good. His name was John something. I have forgotten his surname. He then explained to me the work I had to do. He asked me whether I had a driving licence to drive a tractor. I said "No". He then kept silent for sometime and then went away. After 5 minutes or so he came back with a wheelbarrow.

He then said "Well Arun, there will be lots of metal scraps on the floor. You will have to sweep them, gather them, put them on the wheelbarrow and then take to the dump yard".

He showed me the dump yard, which was about 200 metres away from the factory shed. It was cold outside. My wages were 2DM per hour, which was very low but better than earning nothing. I started to work immediately.

The siren blew at 12 O'clock. So it was lunchtime and all the machines stopped. John suddenly came to me and asked me to go with him for lunch. He would show me the canteen. He brought his own packed lunch. He told me either I could bring my own food and eat here or I could buy the subsidised food from the canteen. He bought a drink and I bought lunch for myself. I had to pay 2DM for the lunch and then left with only 48DM in my pocket. At 12.30 the siren blew again and we all started working again. Everyone was well disciplined and punctual and they never gossiped while working. They all appeared to me like moving machines.

I was doing my job. Collecting all the scrap materials from the shop floor, putting them on the wheelbarrow and then pushing it down to the dump yard 200 metres away. It was freezing cold outside. From next month it would start snowing. I realised I had to take further monetary help from Khokon, the idea of which I didn't like at all.

At 4 O'clock the siren blew and everyone switched off their machine. Everyone was in a hurry to go home. I went to the security office at the exit gate and said my name. The security man then took me to the card-punching machine that records the starting and closing time on the card. He showed me the card and told me what to do with the card when I come for work in the morning and leave the factory after the work. At that time somehow I felt insulted and hurt psychologically. But what could I do ? I was helpless. I punched the card and waited outside the gate for Khokon.

After he came we went together to the clothing shop to buy some warm clothing. I bought a woollen overcoat, two good pullovers and two woollen long underpants. Altogether I had to pay 210DM which Khokon gave me on loan. On our way back I bought a 500 gm packet of sliced white bread, a bottle of Jam, a packet of butter, six eggs and few slices of salami for my breakfast. That would last at least whole of the next week if not longer. I came back home at around 6 O'clock, washed my hands and face and then stretched myself on the bed. Just then both Dolly and Tina entered the room with a pot of coffee and cups & saucers. We had our coffee and some biscuits they brought, though the biscuits were not included in the rent I was paying. Khokon came to my room after we had finished our coffee. He asked me what I would do for dinner. He wanted to know whether I would make some sandwiches or go out for dinner.

I told him "Let us go out for some food. I don't feel like having a full dinner. I would prefer to have something light".

He also felt that way. We went out and had some bread rolls and hot frankfurter sausages. I paid for mine and he paid for his. Then we went out for a stroll, walking silently.

He was the first to break the silence and said "Arun, I know how you are feeling having to work as a factory floor sweeper. I did the same thing here once, now I am a charge-man in the factory. You are a double graduate, Bachelor of Science and Bachelor of Engineer. No one can stop you going up the ladder once you have learnt the language. Talk with the Germans as much as you can and study German in your room after you come back from the work. You will see, within 3 months you will be able to speak the language. Then you will easily find a proper job in your line of profession." After about half an hour of walking, we came back to our rooms.

He was absolutely right as I found out after exactly 3 months.

I prepared my next day's breakfast, two sandwiches and a boiled egg. I kept them on the table well packed. Then I went to the sitting room to watch the TV. The whole Hoffman family was there. At about 10 O'clock I said good night to them and then went for a shower. I had a sound sleep that night.

Next day passed as usual. After I came out from the factory I was thinking what should be done now. I have got only a few Marks in my pocket. I could not afford to go out for food every night. And I was very much reluctant to borrow money from Khokon. As it was, I had to return the 210 DM that I had already received as a loan from him to buy clothes. How could I take a further loan from him for my food? Before Khokon could catch me at the gate of the factory, I quickly walked away from there.

I knew where the shops were. I entered a shop and didn't know what to buy. I did not have much choice. After quick thinking I bought five packets of groundnuts and one tin of prepared food – chicken curry and rice. From there I came back straight to my home. Today also both Dolly and Tina brought coffee and some cakes for all of us. When they kept the tray on the table I took my chair. There was only one chair, so they sat on the bed. I could guess Tina was trying to say something but was not feeling comfortable. Dolly was asking so many questions about work. She heard all about me from Khokon. She encouraged me and said she would teach me German and would not take any fees for that. I was very happy with her proposal. Every day after dinner she would give me lessons for one hour on the language. After some time, Khokon came and asked me whether I would like to go out for any food. I told him that I had something to eat today and if he did not mind I would like to stay at home. He then left and after a while Dolly also left to prepare dinner for them.

When Tina was alone in the room she started talking to me in a very low voice. "Look Arun, I have a boyfriend whom I love very much. My father does not like that I stay out for long hours at night. He wants that I come back definitely before 10 O'clock at night."

I said, "Yes, he is right. At your age you should not stay even that long outside".

She said, "But my friend wants that I spend a few hours with him every evening".

I said, "So, what you want me to do. I can't ask your father on your behalf to allow you to do what you said. He will throw me out of the house. I know your father."

"I have got an idea," she said, "If you keep your window open, no, what I mean is, close the window but do not put the latch on. At night I will go out and come in through the window. No one will ever know about it."

"That means" I said "I will have to keep the door open too. Look, suppose your father got suspicious and entered my room just a second after you have entered my room through that window. That will be very embarrassing - not only for me but for you too. I don't want to listen to any of this – out of here - now".

I was so annoyed with her request that I almost shouted at her. I should not have done that; after all I was a paying guest there. She was naturally very upset. She left the room with a fiery glance at me.

I felt bad and sorry for Tina. I could not agree to her plan. Anyway, why should I bother myself with these things? What bothered me more was that I was feeling hungry. Yesterday I had a dinner that was not so bad, so I wanted to save the tin food I bought. I opened the packet of the groundnuts and started eating. I ate the whole packet and then drank a glass of water. That was my dinner that day. I then prepared two sandwiches and boiled one egg for next day's breakfast. I did not feel like watching the TV. I went out of my room to say good night to the Hoffman family and then came back to my room and went to sleep. I got up at 5 O'clock as usual. I washed my mouth and then shaved. By the time I finished my morning rituals and dressed up Dolly brought a pot of coffee and kept it on the table. I went near the shelf to get my breakfast but I could not find it. I looked around but could not find it anywhere. I could guess who did it but felt it was definitely not fair. I drank the coffee and went to work on an empty stomach.

The day was very colder than any of the previous days. After the day's hard manual labour I came back straight home. Two sandwiches were all that I had eaten the whole day. So after I had my coffee I requested Dolly to warm the tin food I had. After I had finished my dinner, chicken curry and rice, we sat for the language lesson. After about an hour she went to the sitting room to watch the TV and I continued to study the language for another hour. Then I took shower and then prepared the breakfast. This time I kept the breakfast packet under the bed.

Next day passed as usual. I had two sandwiches during lunch. And for dinner I had just a handful of groundnuts and a glass of water. This was going on for three days. On the fourth day, when I was taking my dinner, which was a handful of groundnuts and a glass of water, I could not check myself. I was almost at the verge of weeping. So far I remember I had wept only twice before. Once when my eldest brother died in the year 1950 when I was only 16 years old. And for the second time when my father died in the year 1958 when I was 22 years of age and I was studying in the Engineering College. Now, somehow I checked myself.

I told myself, "Arun, just you wait, tomorrow you will get your hard earned money. Then you can have a hearty dinner. You can have whatever you want to eat."

Next day I got my wages. I still remember it was 65 DM I got in my hand after deducting the Income Tax. I would have to pull on with this the whole of next week and also to repay some amount to Khokon, which I had taken on loan. I waited outside the gate for Khokon and came back home together. That day we had our coffee together. I asked him whether he would like to go to a restaurant for dinner. "Why not" he said, "today we have got our salary".

So around 8 O'clock we went out. We went to a nice cosy restaurant nearby. I ordered Wiener Schnitzel with roast potato and salad and a glass of beer. After the main course we had ice cream too. The schnitzel piece was quite big. After an entire week without a proper dinner that evening I really enjoyed it so much that till today I remember that meal. I paid 6 DM for my food. 6 DM was comparatively costly in those days. I then paid 20 DM to Khokon as a part repayment of the loan.

We came back home at around 11:00 pm. I was bone tired and after having that fabulous dinner I really wanted to go to bed immediately. I hurriedly took a shower and went to sleep. Next day was Saturday and a non-working day. I got up late. I think it was around 10 O'clock in the morning. For the last two days we had not seen the sun. It was cloudy and hazy. They said it was always like that during that time of the year. Next month in November we would be expecting winter snow.

The whole day I did not do anything, just read books and sometimes studied German. In the evening, as usual, after the coffee I went to the sitting room to watch TV. I made it a habit to watch TV not because I liked the programme but to learn the blasted language. I wanted to learn the language as quickly as possible. Dolly of course always encouraged me and said that I was progressing quite well within one week and also said that I had got long way to go. Khokon actually encouraged me to watch TV as much as possible because, what he said was that it would be extremely difficult to learn any language by just reading and studying books. I must hear the language as much as possible.

Three weeks passed. Nothing changed much except that I could then at least converse with someone in German with my limited stock of German vocabulary. On a Monday after three weeks of work as a floor sweeper in the factory, my foreman called me and told me that I need not do the floor sweeping any more. Instead I would work as a machine operator and my wages would be 2.50 DM per hour. He talked to his manager and told him about my progress in the German language. He also knew about my professional qualification and therefore agreed immediately to the recommendation of the foreman. I was ecstatically happy with the news and the happiness was not due to the financial benefit but due to the fact that I need not carry the metal scrap in a wheelbarrow in the snow to the tip which was about 200 metres away from the factory in that biting cold.

The foreman, Mr. John then took me to a machine where I was supposed to work. Another four weeks I worked at that machine and then I was transferred to another section to work with a more sophisticated machine. And for that I was paid at a rate of 3 DM per hour.

At home everything was normal. Dolly was very homely and Tina as usual used to come back home late night but not through the window of my room. She managed to get a duplicate key of the main door. Khokon was deeply in love with a German girl.

It was January 1960. Everywhere there was metre high snow and the temperature, as far as I could remember, was -15 degree C at night and –5 degree C at daytime. On a Friday in the second week of January, the foreman came to me and said that the Director of the company wanted to see me at 4.15 that afternoon. I had met him once earlier with Khokon. In those days in that area of Hagen we were the only Indians. Not only Indians, we two were the only two coloured people. That was why everyone knew us. And

Khokon was very close to the Director. The Director as a person was very friendly and used to like Khokon very much. Khokon also used to visit him regularly. It was only through Khokon I came to know him personally. I came to know later on that he used to keep a watchful eye on me while I was working in the factory.

Exactly at 4.15 I went to the Director's room and reported to his secretary. I was asked to go inside the room as he was waiting for me. It was a day of surprises. He asked me to take a seat. Then he enquired whether I was free the next Saturday in the evening. When I said I didn't have anything to do on that Saturday evening, he invited me for the dinner at his residence. He also said that Khokon was also coming for dinner. He enquired whether I eat beef because he knew I was Hindu and he had to tell his wife accordingly. I told him that I was not very particular about food. In fact I had started eating everything edible.

After hearing that he said, "That's nice, that's nice. So we will meet again tomorrow at about say 6 O'clock evening"

I said, "Yes, I will come tomorrow. It is a great pleasure. See you tomorrow then."

Then I said "Aufwiedersehen" to him and came out of his room.

The whole night I could not sleep. Why had he suddenly invited me? Was it because I was a friend of Khokon or because I was lonely? I am just an ordinary worker in his factory. After breakfast I went to the city centre and spent the whole day wandering around. When I came home it was almost 5 O'clock. I hurriedly took a shower to freshen myself. When I was ready to go, Khokon came to my room in a Black suit. He looked handsome. I had a dark Brown suit and that was the only suit I had. I asked him whether it was OK. He said yes it was fine. So we went out and took a Taxi. The Taxi fare of course he paid. The Director's name was Herr Bock. When we knocked the door, Herr Bock opened the door and welcomed us into his house. We sat in the sitting room. It was fabulously decorated. After a while his wife Frau Bock came to greet us. I presume she was busy in the kitchen.

Picture 7 Mr. and Mrs. Bock

We all sat in the sitting room. Herr Bock asked me about my progress in German language. We started talking in German language. After about 5 minutes he expressed that my knowledge in German Language was good considering

I had not been there long. He hoped that by the end of January I would be able to speak German well enough to work in my professional field. He told me that he heard everything about me from Khokon and would very much like to help me find a proper job if I wished. Alternatively if I wished I could study for a Doctorate in the Aachen Technical Institute. He knew Professor Dr. During of the Institute and he would write a letter to him if I desired. Though I very much wanted to do my Doctorate in there, financially it was not viable. My father had passed away and my younger brother was still studying in Aachen Technical Institute, which required a good amount of money. I explained this to Herr Bock. He asked me to give him all the certificates I had and the other details about me and he would prepare the Resume. Then we discussed about various Electronics firms and prepared a list of preferences. We then sat for dinner. We started with soup and ended with dessert. This was the best dinner that I ever had in Germany. After the dinner we spent about an hour discussing various topics while enjoying a glass of beautiful brandy. The light was dim and the atmosphere was very cosy and friendly.

While discussing various topics he suddenly asked me whether I ate beef against my liking or rather against my religion. I had to explain him that it had nothing to do with religion. In fact it is not clearly mentioned anywhere in our religion that eating beef is prohibited. Then he asked "But Hindus worship Cows and Ox. Is it not so?"

I said "Yes, but the reason is different. We Hindus consider cows are like a mother. You see, a child takes milk from its mother and later on starts drinking cow's milk. We call cows as *Gow Mata* (Gow means Cow and Mata means Mother in Sanskrit)). You see, Hindu religion started forming about 5000 years ago. In those days priests, sages and philosophers propagate knowledge and advice, which has got logic and that common people could understand them easily. Cow milk was and is still today very important food for all of us in this world. If beef was allowed as food then they thought that there could be shortage of milk in future. Therefore Hindus worship Cows. As in Europe Horses were used to plough field, in India Oxen were used to plough field. In fact they are still used in many places in India. Since this action of plough gives us food, they were and are treated as the carrier of God (highest God). Therefore we Hindus worship Ox and don't eat beef. So far what I have told you is according to my knowledge that I have gleaned over time. Others may not agree this viewpoint and may give different explanations.

I also said to Herr Bock that the Hindu religion is not a religion the way western people understand it. Hinduism is a compilation of philosophy which started thousands of year ago, may be 5000 thousand years ago. As you have the Bible for Christians, Koran for Muslims, Granths for the Shikhs, Hindus do not have a single Religion book. We have got *Veda, Ramayana, Mahabharat, Gita (which is of course a part of Mahabharat), Upanishad* etc. And they all are packed with philosophy advising us what to do and what not to do to lead a perfect life. Hinduism (Hindu Philosophy) shows us the way of living."

Since Hinduism is not a Religion but philosophy of life, therefore it is not possible to become a Hindu. However few years ago an organisation started to convert people from other religion or people from no religion to Hindu only and only when they wanted to become Hindu otherwise not.

Herr Bock asked "If Hinduism is not a religion, then how and from where the word "Hinduism" has come."

"This is a very good question" I said. "You see, when Muslims invaded India through Khyber Pass in the North-Western part of Himalaya (known as Hindu Kush Mountain) they first conquered the area which is known as Punjab. (Panjab = Pancha Ab meaning Five Rivers) There are five rivers that flow through Punjab. One of them is known as river Indus and many native people settled there on the bank of that river. They were highly developed both culturally and technologically. When Muslim invaders asked, who they were, the answer was obviously "Oh, they are the people from the Indus valley, they are the Indus." Later on the word "Indus" became "Hindus" and the philosophy of life followed by those people was termed as Hinduism. The Muslims started addressing them as Hindus and later on officially recorded Hinduism as religion. Even the word "India" came from the name of the river Indu. The actual name of India was Bharat, after the name of the King Bharat who ruled the land thousands of years ago.

After spending few more hours with them and discussing various topics, we came back home around 10 O'clock.

Next day I prepared a short life history of mine and got it typed. On Monday morning I went straight to Herr Bock's room and handed over the history sheet to him. He smiled at me and told me not to worry, everything will be all right. Next day he called me in his room and gave me the Resume and a draft of the covering letter. He gave me a list of five leading Electronics Companies in Germany. He asked me to get the covering letter typed by his secretary, signed the letter and enclosed all the copies of the certificates. The applications were given to his secretary for posting. After about a week I got reply from all the five companies. Three companies had called me for an interview. Other two companies had sent the appointment letters stating all the terms and conditions and the salary range. I could imagine they were in dire need of engineers. However, I preferred the interview from Siemens Company since it is an International Company and it has a very big establishment in India. In case if I decided to go back to India it would be easy if I worked for Siemens. They would reimburse the train fare, hotel and other expenses. After I received the replies, I immediately went to see Herr Bock for further discussion. I expressed my wish to join Siemens Company and explained why. He gladly agreed to that.

He looked at the interview date and said, "Arun, you have got only seven days in hand. Today is Tuesday; send a telex advising them that you will be there on Thursday morning at 10 O'clock for the interview."

He then didn't wait for me to send the Telex. He himself dictated the telex to his secretary and also asked her to buy a return train ticket to Munich.

He then looked at me and said, "This will be the presentation from the Bock family".

"But" I said, "The fare will be reimbursed by Siemens".

"Well, then," he said, "this is a bonus payment from this company for the good and hard work done by you. Your job here is terminated today. Go home, take rest and prepare yourself for the interview. Tomorrow morning you come here and collect from the personnel department the balance payment and another extra two weeks payments in lieu of notice".

Next day was Wednesday; I boarded the Munich bound train in the evening. It was an overnight journey. Next day early morning I reached Munich. I didn't travel in the Sleeper compartment, so when I got down from the train my whole body felt like a giant ache. My eyes were also burning due to a sleepless night. First I went to the Men's Room, washed my face and tidied up. I had a quick breakfast at the Milk Bar inside the Railway Station. While I was taking my break fast I enquired how to go to the Siemens Central Laboratory in Hoffman Strasse. I was told that there was a direct tramcar from the station to Hoffman Strasse.

When I reached there it was only 8 O'clock and my interview was at 10 O'clock in the morning. I entered the building complex through the main gate and then went to the front desk. There was no receptionist at that hour but the Watchman came forward and enquired. I showed him the interview letter. He gave me a very friendly welcoming smile. He then escorted me to the fourth floor and then through many zigzagging corridors to a well decorated office room. The secretary was in the front room of the office. The Manager there was in charge of five laboratories. If successful at the interview, I would be working for him in one of his laboratories.

I gave the interview letter to the secretary. She read it and asked me to take a chair. She smiled and then enquired, "Why have you come so early? It is only 8.15 now and your interview is at 10 O'clock."

I told her "The train from Hagen reached Munich in the early morning. Well, what shall I do now? Outside it is too cold and its also snowing."

She laughed for a few seconds and then said, "Well, you can wait here. You can take off your overcoat and relax."

I think she enjoyed my German language more than anything else did. I gave her my overcoat. She put it inside a side cupboard. She then prepared a cup of coffee for me. After about half an hour or so, a middle aged bald headed person entered the room. She got up and introduced me to him. He was the boss. His name was Hr. Bandel. He then guided me inside his office room. Since I had already come here he said he could take the formal interview now. After about an hour of questioning on various subjects and interviewing thoroughly he enquired when I could join.

I said, "I will have to go back to Hagen, pack my things and come back again. So 1st of February as a joining date will be suitable."

He looked at the calendar and said, "1st February is a Sunday. So you join us on 2nd of February. Your salary will be 700DM per month to start with and you will be appointed as a Laboratory Engineer in Grade 4. Is it all right for you?

At first I could not believe it. Did I hear correctly? I stammered and said' "Yes Sir"

And thanked him very much. 700DM per month salary in those days (in 1960) was not bad at all. After all I was alone and that was only the starting salary.

He then took me to the Laboratory where I would be working. That Laboratory was doing research and development on Remote Control and Remote Supervision System in the field of Telecommunications. Mr. Bandel then introduced me to the Chief of that laboratory. His name was Mr George Gluender. We three had a small discussion on the type of work I would do in that laboratory. Mr. Bandel then left for his office. Mr Gluender then took me around his laboratory and also to the other four laboratories. These five laboratories worked in a group under Mr. Bandel. When we were finished with this "conducted tour" of the laboratories it was 12.30 pm. I was really feeling hungry. Mr. Gluender then rang Mr. Bandel and then proceeded towards the Guest Canteen. Mr. Bandel was already there when we reached the Guest Canteen. We occupied a table.

I was asked what drink I would like to have. There was a set menu for the day and the choice was only for the drink. I was a bit hesitant because I was not sure about the type of drinks allowed here. I told them to choose whatever they liked because I did not know what drinks were available there. They then ordered a bottle of wine. Only Wine and beer were served in the Guest Canteen and not available in the General Canteen.

After we had finished our lunch Mr. Bandel gave me a payment voucher for the 1st class return train fare, return taxi fare from station to work and a day's expense. I was to collect the money from the cashier on the ground floor of the main building. I shook hands with them and said 'Aufwiedersehen' feeling a mixture of relief, gratefulness, joy and bemusement at my good fortune.

When I reached the station it was about 3 O'clock. The train for Hagen was to leave at 6 O'clock. I already had the return ticket in economy class, which Mr Bock had given to me in Hagen. I went to the reservation counter and got my seat reserved. I had enough time on my hands and therefore went to a restaurant in the station and had some coffee. Later I bought dinner packet for the night.

I reached Hagen next day early morning. I gave the news to the Hoffman family. They were very happy to hear the news, but they didn't like me going away from Hagen. In the evening I broke the news to Khokon who was very happy for me. I met Mr. Bock in the same evening at his residence. He was very very happy when I told him that I got a job in their Central Laboratory as a Laboratory Engineer. I told him the salary they had offered. He said that it was a good salary to start with. He was so happy that he wanted to know in great detail how the interview went and all about the Research Laboratory, and the work I will have to do and I gladly told him all.

I left Hagen on 1ˢᵗ of February by the evening train. It was very painful to leave Hagen. After all, I had spent so many days there with the Hoffmans, Khokon and the Bocks. I knew I would never come back to Hagen because Hagen was a steel city and my work would be in the field of Electronics. When I left home in the afternoon to catch the train I saw tears in Tina's eyes. Tina was very naughty but I knew she had a very soft heart. I think my eyes were also wet.

6

SUN SHINE DAYS IN GERMANY

I reached Munich early in the morning on 2nd February 1960. It was a very cold morning. In fact the winter was severe in Europe in 1960; especially Munich which had it's the coldest winter in 50 years. When I came out of the Railway Station, everything was covered with snow. The beautifully decorated Christmas tree was still there in the open space in front of the Station. The tree was about 8 to 10 metres high. Though it was morning, the sun would rise at around 8 O'clock. All the streetlights were on. The Christmas lights on the tree were also on. Everything was dazzling in the light because of freshly fallen pure white snow. I came out of the station building, shivering in the cold and walked slowly towards the Tramcar Stop. I had to wait for about 15 to 20 minutes freezing in that cold weather. The office hour's rush had not started. Inside the tramcar it was warm. I put my feet on the heater, which was on the side of the car. It took about 45 minutes to reach my destination. Again I had to walk on the snow from the Tram Stop to the Siemens complex, which was about a Kilometre in distance. I was always wondering how people could live in such freezing weather while all the time missing the heat of the Indian sun. But later on I acclamatised and really enjoyed winter in Munich.

When I reached Siemens, it was about 7:00 in the morning. I went straight to the person who stood near the front desk and showed him my appointment letter. He then guided me to the laboratory where I would be working. I saw Mr Gluender in the laboratory. He came forward and welcomed me. He then introduced me to the other colleagues in the laboratory. Other than the boss of the laboratory Mr. Gluender and I there were three more Laboratory Engineers. After about six months or so our team grew in strength to 8 Engineers. Though everyone was very friendly, helpful and accommodative, I liked Mr. Gerhard Sager most of all. I do not know the reason but our friendship grew stronger. He was about 10 years older than I. He used to look after me like my elder brother. I also respected him as he always guided me in the right direction. His wife was also working in the same central laboratory complex but in another laboratory. Her name was Erika. At lunchtime she used to come to our laboratory. She and Gerd used to go for lunch together. I used to go for lunch alone, sometimes with other colleagues.

On the day before the Easter Holidays, we had a small Tea Party in the Boss's room. As usual we were discussing various topics. Someone raised the topic of Suttee burning in India by Hindus.

So I started explaining the whole thing as follows:

"Suttee (In Sanskrit Sati, that is 'True Wife') is a practice that prevailed in India of a widow burning herself on the funeral Pyre, either with the body of her husband or, if he had died at a distance, separately.

Classical authors mention it as early as 316 BC. In theory the act of suttee was voluntary, but in orthodox communities any woman who refused to perform it was excluded from the society. Burning of widows on the funeral Pyre is no where mentioned in Hindu religion. It became more of a custom rather than anything to do with religion. It became more common after the invasion of India by the Muslims during the 16ᵗʰ/17ᵗʰ century.

Pathans and Moguls came to India through the Khyber Pass in the North-Western part of Himalayas. In those days India was ruled by many kings and Maharajas. There was practically no war or fighting between these kings. all of India was very peaceful. Hence the solders did not have any experience of war. When Muslim invaders attacked various kingdoms, the soldiers were literally slaughtered. Thereby thousands of married women became widows. Many of them were by force taken to Harems for entertainment. And many widows of the fallen solders decided to commit suicide by throwing themselves on the Pyre rather than leading a life in Harem as a prostitute. Ultimately the invaders conquered almost whole of India. Later on, especially in villages, the Head person or the Brahmins priests insisted rather made a rule that widows must be burnt alive along with her dead husband on the Pyre. This was more due to greed than anything else since a dead woman had no claim to her husband's property and also needed no looking after.

The custom was abolished by the British in 1829, but isolated instances persisted in remote parts of India until the early 1900s".

Slowly I started making friendships in Munich. I had both German friends and Indian friends. My closest friend amongst the Indians was Ghosh Dastidar. I used to call him Ghosh. He was also working in Siemens laboratory but his laboratory was about 10 Kilometre away from my work place. We used to meet each other almost on all weekends. He had a car and very often on weekends we used to drive away from the city. He used to live in a one-room apartment house, which had a small kitchen. He used to cook Indian dishes and naturally I used to go to his place very often for weekend lunches.

Ghosh came to Germany about 4 to 5 years before I came to Germany. He could speak fluent German. I once asked him how he could learn such a tough language so well in such a short time.

He said, "Oh, from Long Haired Dictionary. You should also manage one if you want to learn the language quickly."

At first I did not understand what he meant by Long Haired Dictionary. But then when I understood that he meant girlfriends I said, "No, I do not want any 'Long Haired Dictionary'. They talk too much. I am living with a German family and in the laboratory I am surrounded by the Germans, so I can learn the language without your so called 'dictionary'. In any case I do not want to marry any German Girl.

You see, we have grown up in a different society, in a different culture. We have a different language and different food habits. Everything is different. Can you mix oil and water together? You can put them in a bottle, shake them vigorously as much as you wish, and keep them for some time, you will see they are separated again."

However now I have changed my views about this mixing of Oil and Water. My younger brother, Barun, married a German girl and they had a very good marriage. He settled in Germany. But unfortunately he passed away in 2012 – but after leading a very happy life with his wife and daughters.

I know Ghosh didn't marry any German girl either.

I was staying as a paying guest with a German family. I was paying DM50.00 per week for the room. After a year or so I moved to another house with a bigger room. For this room I was paying the same rent.

Picture 8 In my room in Munich with 2 friends

The landlady was an elderly woman and used to treat me like her son. The house was not far from my work place and it used to take about 15 minutes by bus to reach there. In my room I had a single bed, a sofa set, a wardrobe, one writing table with a chair and one big table with drawers at one corner of the room. This table I used to prepare breakfast and to warm up food. Later I bought an electric hotplate and some kitchen utensils to prepare simple Indian dishes. Ghosh used to come sometimes for weekend lunches.

The landlady was a widow and had one son. Her son used to live in Munich but during my stay there I hardly saw him. Every month on a particular day she used to go to the cemetery, which was near to our house, and lay flowers on her husband's grave. Once she was very sick and could not go out for a month. So, without her knowledge I went to the cemetery on that particular day and put a bunch of red roses on her husband's grave. Next day she was comparatively well and managed to go to the cemetery. I did not know that. After I came back from my work I prepared two cups of coffee and went to the landlady's room. I placed a cup of coffee in front of her and started drinking my coffee. I asked her how she was feeling now. She looked at me straight into my eyes without blinking.

She then asked me, "Arun did you go to the cemetery yesterday?"

I said, "Why? Why are you asking this?"

She asked me again, this time little louder, "Did you go to the cemetery yesterday? Did you put some roses on his grave?"

I kept silent. My head was down. I did not know what to say. Did I do something wrong? Was it not allowed? Or, was it unethical? Then I raised my head and looked at her eyes. I saw tears rolling down her cheeks.

Just for a second I thought my mother was sitting in front of me. In subconscious mind I uttered "Mutter" (Mother in English). After that day I used to call her Mutter and I was treated like her son. I became one of her family. I also started doing household work, which was difficult for her to carry out because of her age. For example floor (carpet) cleaning, carrying the garbage bag to the bin, paying telephone bills and electricity bills at the post office etc.

I remember, before I left Germany for India, she requested me to stay with her. Stay with her forever like her son. She wanted someone on whom she could depend, someone who would look after her as she was quite old. But this was not possible for me. This request I could not accept. I had to go back to my home country due to various personal reasons. The departure was really very painful. Her son hardly used to visit her. She did not have anyone else in this world to look after her. She was very lonely. I wished I could stay with her forever, but alas, I could not do that.

In the meantime my friendship with Gerhard and Erika grew. I started visiting their house often. Of course most of the time Gerhard used to take me to their house in his car and again drop me back to my place. I remember, once we - Gerhard, Erika and myself, went to Switzerland to see a model plane flying competition. At that time they had a very small two-seater car; the name of the model of that car was Ijeta (or Izeta).

Picture 9 On our way to Zurich from Munich in a 2 seater Ijeta

We all cramped inside the car and drove for twelve hours. The maximum speed the car could attain was only 60KM per hour. On the way we stopped for an hour to take some food. They brought some sandwiches with them for all of us and I brought one dozen boiled eggs.

Seeing one dozen boiled eggs, both Gerhard and Erika laughed and said, "What shall we do with one dozen boiled eggs?"

I said, "Why, we will eat them naturally."

They ate four eggs and I alone ate eight eggs though not all at once.

Anyway we reached Switzerland safely and enjoyed the model plane flying show and the competition. It was about 5 O'clock when the show and the competition were over. We started our return journey towards Munich. When we reached Lindau, Gerd got an idea. We were cramped in the small car and it was very uncomfortable. He suggested that I travel in the train from Lindau to Munich. He will fetch me from the Munich railway station and would drop me at my home. Idea was not bad. He dropped me at the Lindau railway station. I looked at my watch and the train timetable, which was on one of the walls in the station. There was still 2 to 3 minute's time left for the train to catch. I waved my hands to Gerhard and ran towards the ticket counter. I hurriedly bought a ticket to Munich and ran towards the platform. I did not realise that the train was at the far end of the station. When I reached the platform the train had just left the platform and I could see the tail lamp of the train. Then I again ran towards the entrance gate of the station with a hope to catch Gerhard. But by that time he had already left. I entered the station again and enquired at the ticket counter when the next train to Munich would leave. He said, "The next train will leave tomorrow in the early morning at 6 O'clock". I looked at the ticket; it had today's date. I asked whether I could travel tomorrow with that ticket because I missed the last train to Munich. He said, "Yes, But you are allowed to travel only by the first train of the day". So I was left alone in the station. After paying for the ticket I did not have enough money to stay in a hotel for the night. And the station would be closed after the last train left. I explained to the stationmaster my situation and requested him to allow me to stay in the waiting room for the night. He was very kind and allowed me to stay in the waiting room for the night. He informed the security guard about my stay in the waiting room and then left the station. At around 11 O'clock the security guard came to me and told that there was a phone call for me. He led me to the phone. Gerhard rang from the Munich station. He said he was very sorry that I missed the train. He never thought that I would miss the train. He promised to pick me up from Munich station next morning. Since then our friendship grew faster.

It was an experience to spend a whole night without sleep in a Railway Station waiting room. Off and on the security man came to me and enquired about me. He told me that Lindau is a beautiful small town at Boden See (Lake of Konstanz). Many tourists come here during summer to spend their holidays. Then I decided, that, yes, I would definitely come here once and spend few days. Gerhard came next day morning to Munich station to receive me and then dropped me off to my place.

One day my friend Ghosh suggested going for a long drive and spending the coming long weekend somewhere away from Munich's crowd. When he suggested Lindau, I immediately agreed. I told him that I spent one night in Lindau but I didn't elaborate. Lindau is a nice small town. Many holidaymakers come to Lindau to spend few days there. It is situated at one end of the Konstanz Lake. Three countries, Germany, Austria and Switzerland surround this lake. We stayed in Lindau, which is in Germany. We went to Bregrenz in Austria, and to Friedricks Hafen in Switzerland. All these places are along the lake. From Friedricks Hafen we went to St Gallen. We criss-crossed the lake many times to our heart's content and really enjoyed our weekend holiday.

In this way whenever an opportunity presented itself I travelled anywhere in Europe. Amongst the big cities I visited were Paris, Venice, London, Rome, Vatican City, Stockholm, Vienna, Berlin, Frankfurt, Erlangen, Hamburg, and many small holiday resorts on the Alps.

Though I have seen many Museums and other architectural marvels in the big cities, the natural beauty of the Alps are unforgettable. Whenever I got time I used to drive to the Alps. It is so wonderful in summer to see the snow clad mountain peaks and the lovely greens on the plain land and in the valley. There are many villages and towns in the valleys of the Alps. The food in these villages or towns is fabulously tasty and authentic. The people in these mountain villages are also very friendly and genuine.

I also used to go from Munich to the nearby big lakes. One is 'Ama Lake' and the other is 'Stanberger Lake'. I went often and saw people sailing or just roaming around along the shore enjoying the fresh air.

I liked the natural beauty of the Alps and the Black Forest. The drive along the Rhein River was so beautiful that each time I was left with a feeling of wonder. The small towns through which you drive along the Rhein River are postcard pretty. There are few forts and palaces which are worth seeing. I liked this journey so much that I did this twice and if I given a chance will do it once again.

I loved German cuisine and I still do. My most favourite dishes were Wiener Schnitzel with baked potato and peas, Schwinebraten or Schwine Kotellete with mashed potato and beans and Apple juice.

In Paris I thought of trying some beefsteak and red wine, which Paris was famous for during those days. When I ordered the waitress asked me what kind of steak I would like to have, I said I would like to have medium. After about fifteen minutes she brought the food. I cut a piece from the steak and was about to put it in my mouth. I saw to my horror that blood drops were just dripping out of the piece of meat. If that was medium then what would rare be like?

Two years passed. I was enjoying my work in the laboratory. After a year and half of working hard, I had the good fortune of being able to invent a design of a Decade Counter using Transistors and Ferrite Cores which was patented in my name on behalf of Siemens AG. I was recognised as an inventor in West Germany. After that I was awarded the highest grade as a Laboratory Engineer.

Time was passing and I was enjoying every day of my stay in Munich. I used to visit Gerhard and Erika very often. I remember it was the third week of December 1960 when Gerhard invited me for dinner to his house on Christmas Eve. I went to their house with a bunch of flowers and a gift. On that day I met Erika's elder sister Ingrid (in short Inge) and her mother. They both were very nice to me. Seeing them I felt very home sick. My mother and sisters were so far away from Munich. May be Gerhard and Erika felt that I was lonely and that was the reason why they gave me the precious gift of their company often. Slowly I became like one of their family. Inge lived in Munich but in a separate house. Once, I think it was in 1994; she came to Australia on holidays with her girl friend and stayed with us in Sydney for three days. Now Inge is 86 years of age. In 1996 she moved to an Old People's Home. Gerhard and Erika have built their own house in a suburb of Munich called Germering. Inge's Old People's Home is not far from the place where Gerhard and Erika live. It is very unfortunate that Gerhard passed away year before last (2012)

While we were enjoying the Christmas Eve dinner, Gerhard asked whether we celebrate Christmas in India. I said, "Yes of course. There are many Christians in India. They celebrate as you celebrate Christmas here in Europe. But Hindus and the rest of the people in India celebrate in different ways. Because of the Christmas and the New Year Holidays, streets and houses are illuminated; and people go out for dinner and they dance the whole night. This festivity starts around the middle of December and continues till the beginning of January. This is particularly true in Calcutta. Especially Park Street in Calcutta which becomes a place of attraction due to its lights, restaurants, cake shops and pastries.

Picture 10 Park Street in Calcutta during Christmas and New Year

Picture 11 Park Street in Calcutta during Christmas and New Year

Erika asked, "What are the religious functions you observe in India, I mean by Hindus.

"Oh many", I said "They are different in different parts in India."

"In the eastern region especially in Bengal we celebrate 'Durga Puja' (worship of Goddess Durga, Goddess who destroys all evil), 'Saraswati Puja (worship of Goddess Swaraswati, Goddess of learning), Shiva Puja (worship of Supreme God Shiva who is the destroyer as well as the creator of all), Lakshmi Puja (Worship 0f Goddess Lakshmi, Goddess of wealth) and Ganesh Puja (worship of God Ganesh, God of business and prosperity) and Kali Puja (Kali is the goddess associated with Shakti or power).

In other parts of India there are different religious events in addition to what I have mentioned above."

Gerhard told "Yes, I have heard that Hindus have many God and Goddess"

I said "Yes, of course. We have one hundred and eight Gods and Goddesses. And there are many advantages too to have so many Gods and Goddess"

"And what are they?" Gerhard and Erika both enquired.

I jokingly said "Say there are 2000 people from various parts of India asking simultaneously for immediate help. This way the Gods and Goddesses will not be perpetually overworked and everyone can get their help on time. If you have only one God what will He do alone? India has a huge population."

They all started laughing.

I used to go very often to their house. Sometimes they used to take me on long drives to various villages in the Alps region.

I had a very small friend circle and often found myself with too much time on my hands. Gerhard advised me to take up some hobby. At that time Gerhard used to fly remote controlled model glider planes. I got some inspiration from him and then one day I bought a kit of a remote controlled model plane. I then started making the radio control system in the laboratory where I was working. The remote control system consists of a radio transmitter and a receiver. But this project of mine remained unfinished. I could not complete them and my plane never took off. I started with much interest, but the interest disappeared very quickly. May be because I was too lonely and I lost the urge to do anything interesting.

I bought a car. It was a second hand junk but good enough for city driving. Once Ghosh and I drove more than 150 Kilo-metre at a stretch in that old junk. The car was not that bad! Whenever I got time I used to just drive away from the city or meet my friends and Gerhard. The comfort of having a car in Munich was great since it afforded a certain independence and security. I no longer needed to depend on public transport or borrowed rides from friends. I did not need to wait at the Tram or Bus Stop in the cold windy weather or drizzling summer. I did not need to wear heavy overcoats or raincoats when I went for weekend dances. I used to go dancing once in a month with my friends, especially with Ghosh.

One day my brother who was studying in Aachen Technical Institute came to Munich with his two friends on week long holiday. I asked them to stay with me. I took permission from my landlord so they could stay in my room. My brother slept on the couch and his two friends slept on the floor on air mattresses, which they brought along with them. I took them around the city and to the famous museums and Palaces in Munich. Though it was a holiday for them, for me it was a big change; a change from a monotonous life. After they left I became more attached to the Gerhard family and looked forward to spending time with them more often.

Erika gave birth to a baby girl. She was cute and very lovely. My visit to them became more frequent. Her name is Petra. Now she is a doctor and practising in a nearby town.

Three years had passed and I was planning to come back to India. I expressed my wish to my boss. Within a few months the opportunity came and I jumped up to take it. Siemens India was looking for an Engineer and I was selected. I had to take six months special training before I could leave Germany for India. One month before my departure I sent all my belongings to Calcutta by ship. Siemens Germany arranged shipment of my luggage. After about ten days or so the personnel department from the Siemens Head Office informed me that my luggage had been broken into at Genoa and some of the contents were stolen. The luggage was kept in the shipping company's transit store. Fortunately the luggage was insured. I was asked to go to Genoa immediately to identify the items that were stolen. I was given a return rail ticket to Genoa by Siemens and was told that a day's hotel expense and the incidental expenses will be reimbursed to me. Telex message was sent to the insurance company providing details of my arrival in Genoa.

The train journey from Munich to Genoa was spectacular. It was mid January and the winter was really severe during that time of the year. Snow was everywhere and the ground was white. The train left Munich station at night. I looked outside through the window. Trees and meadows were all covered with dazzling white snow. I do not remember when I fell asleep. In the morning when I got up, the train was already running on the Alps. The scenery was extraordinary. The mountains, the forest, the valleys and those little waterfalls, everything was so beautiful that it felt like it was God's country. Everything was covered by sparkling white snow. The beauty can only be felt and enjoyed. It is difficult for an engineer like me who thinks in terms of facts and figures to describe the joy I felt at seeing such beauty.

After washing I went to the dining car to have my breakfast. It was around noon when I reached Genoa. An Italian gentleman came to the station to receive me. I was taken to his office to complete the formalities. I gave him the list of contents of the luggage. Then we went to their transit store where my luggage was kept. The inspector then checked the list with the belongings and prepared a list of missing items. We came back to his office, had coffee (it was strong Italian coffee) and an hour of mild chit-chat. later I received a packet of money containing German Marks. The amount was much more than what I paid for those lost items. It might be that the calculation was on the basis of the Italian market price of those items I lost. He then gave me a lift to the Railway Station. I took the night train so as to reach Munich next day at noon.

I was the only passenger in the compartment where I took my seat. It was cold. I saw a lever beneath the window. On one side of the lever it was written 'Fredo' and on the other side 'Kaldo'. I thought Kaldo meant cold and Fredo naturally would mean "Fire" or for that matter "Hot". So I pushed the lever to Fredo. Half an hour passed and it was still shivering cold. Then the Ticket Checker came and I showed him the ticket. He punched the ticket, then looked at me and then put the heating lever on the Kaldo. He smiled at me and left the compartment. I was very much annoyed by his behaviour. I was shivering in cold and that fellow came here and pushed the heating lever to Kaldo. I pushed the lever back to Fredo and waited for the compartment to be heated up. After about half an hour or so as he was passing through my compartment he saw me shivering in cold and looked at the heating lever. He came to me and then asked me whether I was feeling cold.

I said, "Are you joking? If I am to stay here like this for another one hour, I will be dead meat."

He then told me in his Italian English, "That is heater handle (showing me the lever). Put it in Fredo it cools down. Put it in Kaldo it hots up. Fredo means cold, freeze, and Kaldo means hot."

He then shifted the lever to the Kaldo position, smiled at me and then left the compartment. I most probably looked like a banana and waited for the compartment to heat up which it did within half an hour. That Ticket Checker came again to my compartment to make sure that I didn't play with the heater lever again. I was very tired and I did not know when I fell asleep in that cosy warm compartment. When I got up it was morning. I looked outside. The sky was covered with white clouds, which meant it wouldn't snow. It would take another 3 to 4 hours to reach Munich.

After reaching Munich I went straight to my apartment. I was so tired I didn't feel like going to work. Next day I reported in detail to the personnel department. They asked me to collect the Air ticket to India next week. They had booked my flight on 31st of January 1963 and I was to report Head office in Bombay on 2nd of February.

Since that day I was on leave. The only job I had was to attend all my farewell dinners at my friend's houses and at Gerhard's place. Gerhardd, Erika, Petra, Ghosh and few more friends came to the Munich Airport to see me off. I felt sad leaving Germany. When I had left India 3 and half years ago I was sad but not so much because I knew I would come back to India again. But now I didn't know whether I would come back to Germany again to meet my friends here specially Gerhard, Erika, Petra and Inge. (I was lucky; I went to Germany/Europe seven times afterwards).

One thing I have learned is that human civilisation is based on the philosophy of 'Give and Take'. This is the very essence of human society. You get what you give and vice versa.

7

BACK TO INDIA

I landed safely in Bombay on 1st of February 1962. It was Sunday. This was my first time in Bombay now called Mumbai. I knew no one there. From the Airport I went directly to the centre of the city and checked in at a hotel which was booked by Siemens Germany. I assumed that the Siemens Indian Head Office would be in the heart of the city. Next morning I took my shower, had my breakfast and then went out of the hotel to catch a taxi. I came to the office and showed my transfer letter from Germany to the receptionist. She welcomed me and said that my boss at New Delhi was waiting for me. She then directed me to the Personnel department where I completed all the formalities. I was then asked to go to the hotel and take rest and come back next day morning to collect the Air ticket to New Delhi.

So I reached New Delhi the next day afternoon. My trip to Delhi was also a first. The taxi driver of the taxi I caught the next morning informed me that the Siemens Office was in

Cannought Place. It would be hardly a 50 metre walk. But by taxi it would be about 1KM drive due to the one-way traffic. I thanked the driver, got out of the taxi and walked down the road. It took me hardly 5 minutes.

The same thing happened to me once in Paris. I was staying in a hotel at Pigalle. After the city sight seeing in buses and underground trains I got down at Pigalle underground train station. I was so tired I thought I would better take a taxi. After I came out from the station I got into a taxi straight away. I told the driver the name of the hotel I was staying. Presumably the driver spoke only French. So he did not speak a single word instead he got down from the Taxi, came around and opened the door and signalled me to get down from the Taxi in a polite manner. When I got down from the Taxi, he pointed out his finger to a high rise building. I looked at the building and saw the big neon sign on the top of it. It was the hotel where I was staying. He gave me a big smile, saluted me and then got into his Taxi. I looked like a banana again.

So I entered the Siemens India office and introduced myself. They already knew about my arrival. I started my new life in India. In Germany I was working in the Research and Development Laboratory and now I would be working as a Project Engineer. It was an absolutely new type of work but I ended up enjoying it.

Then after six months or so, our company got a Development order from the Ministry of Defence, Government of India. Its work was to develop a Mobile Short-wave Radio Station. Further details I cannot give due to the Oath of Secrecy

I took then. Since I had a good experience in this area, I was chosen by the management to take full responsibility of development and produce a prototype. I was then temporarily transferred to Madras City because one of the Government factories in Madras would manufacture the prototype according to our design. I spent six months there to design the Short Wave Mobile Station that suited Indian requirement and then produced the prototype. The prototype had to be completed within six months. I had to work long hours - almost 18hours a day to complete the project. The prototype would be tried in Delhi and also in the mountainous region near Kashmir.

The prototype Mobile Wireless Station was soon ready and we tried all the modes of operation like Voice, Telex and Fax. The trial was successful.

Picture 12 In front of the Wireless mobile Station

Picture 13 Supervising the installation of Whip Antenna

In the mean time I went more than twice to Calcutta on a week's holiday each time. My marriage was fixed on 14th of December 1963.

The prototype was supposed to be tried during that time. To get leave at that time was out of question. My boss and the Managing Director would never agree to that. The invitation cards for the marriage were printed and posted. I hinted to my boss about my marriage date and he strongly suggested postponing my marriage. My boss and the Managing Director were Germans and they would not realise the difficulties regarding postponing the date of marriage. The person in charge for the trial of prototype was one Colonel X, who became Brigadier shortly afterwards. (I can not disclose the real name due to obvious reasons). I then once went to his Office, which was within the Army compound and unburdened my problem with dates.

I told him "Sir, you know how difficult it is to postpone the marriage when everything has been finalised. I will have to be in Calcutta latest by 12th of December and from there I can go to Delhi only after 20th. The company is after the business and will not understand my difficulties".

He was about 45 years of age and I was at that time only 27 years old. He said, "Mr. Sarkar, Do not worry, it is not a problem. The prototype Mobile Station has to be driven from here to New Delhi. I will have to arrange a special team for the trial run of the Mobile station. I will fix up a trial date say 22nd of December. Will it be all right for you?"

I said, "Yes, but why not fix it up after the Christmas."

He said, "OK, I will fix up the trial date on and from 27th of December. I will advise your company to-morrow accordingly. You apply for your leave only after 2 or 3 days". I was very grateful to him for postponing the trial date of the prototype Mobile Station.

8

MY MARRIAGE

I was married on 14 December 1963. My wife's name is Malabika, in short Mala. It took three days according to all our Bengali rites and rituals to complete the marriage ceremony. It is not so in other parts of India. In Bengal marriage can be a tedious job.

On the first day bridegroom must take bath/shower with turmeric paste which is prepared fresh on that morning. This is said to purify the body and make it beautiful. The turmeric paste is kept in a bowl. The groom uses half of the paste and the remaining half is sent to the bride's house for her shower/bath. (Turmeric is root that is used as a medicine and also a spice.

Turmeric is an essential ingredient of the Curry powder. In marriage we use turmeric because according to me after marriage men get cooked. On a serious note the bowl carrying the turmeric paste can be made of clay, brass, copper, silver or gold depending upon how well to do the groom's side of the family are. But traditionally the bowl is made of clay. The bowl containing the turmeric paste is then received by a married woman preferably a relative of the bride. All the married women in the bride's family start applying the turmeric paste all over her and feed the bride some milk-based sweets. The bride then takes her shower/bath .

The bride's house is decorated with lights from a day or two before the day of marriage. The flower decorations are of course made on the day of marriage. The bride's guardian sends a car decorated with flowers (in olden days it was a horse driven carriage) to bring the groom from his house. The marriage takes place in the bride's house. The groom is then escorted to bride's house by his relatives and friends. This could be a convoy of cars carrying fifty to hundred people depending upon the size of the family, near relatives and the friends. The groom's party is then received by the bride's guardians or by her elderly relatives. My future father- in-law had had a huge tent erected on the lawn in front of their house. It was well decorated and a good number of chairs were there for the guests to take their seats.

The wedding dinner was lavish and consisted of ten to twelve courses with sweet dishes and coffee/tea. Because there were a few European guests (my father-in-law was working in a British Bank as a Chief Accountant) a separate enclosure for hard drinks was arranged. Of course a few other Indian guests had well utilised this facility.

The actual marriage started at around 10:00 pm. There were two priests; one from our side and the other priest was from the bride's side. They started chanting Mantras in front of the Pyre (Fire God). Then I had to utter few Mantras and so did the bride. (She was still then not my wife). We had to read Mantras in front of "Narayan Sheela" the supreme God. The bride is then literally carried on a wooden platform, which is carried seven times around the groom. (It is said that by so doing the wife will not be able get out of the marriage knot and will be wife of that person for the next seven consecutive life, (wishful thinking indeed). Then the groom applies sindoor which is vermillion - a red powder and the sign of marriage, at the parting of hair on the bride's head and also a red spot at the middle of her two eyebrows or at the centre of her forehead. This is called a bindi or a tip. The priests then declare them as husband and wife.

Hold on. Hold on! The marriage is still not over. I told you earlier that it takes three days to complete. All the actual wedding rituals ended around 1AM. We were then taken to a room where we supposed to spend our night amongst three to four kids and with two younger cousin sisters of my wife. That is the custom. We were not left alone. This gathering is called "Bashor". Usually the bride and the groom's family have a lot of fun at the expense of the bride and the groom – teasing them and asking impossible riddles.

Mala, who was then only 18 years old, was all chatting away with her cousins. I was not interested in their gossip and dozed away at the time. All the time I was half-awake and half-asleep. I do not remember when I fell asleep. It was about 8 O'clock morning when I suddenly got up. I saw we were five persons on the bed and all of them were fast asleep. Anyway, later on breakfast was served. At around 12 noon people started pouring in. They all came to bless the newly wedded couple. At around 2PM my elder brother and my brother-in-law (Husband of my elder sister) came to take us home, our home.

When we came to our home, the house was fully decorated with lights and coloured cloths. This was the second day. We got down from the car and my mother was there to receive us.

After we had finished our lunch my new wife and me were separated. She was taken to one side of the house and I was asked to go to the other side of the house and I was not supposed to even see her before the sunrise on the next day. This is the custom in Bengal, which has been followed for centuries. I knew about this and the story that goes with it. It is like this:

'A newlywed couple after their marriage went to a secluded hut to spend their second night there. On that night when they were fast asleep a snake entered their room and bit the man. He died instantly. When the woman got up in the morning she saw her husband lying dead. She saw the bite mark of the snake'.

I am not going further on details, but this is the reason why on the second day after wedding the husband and the wife are separated for the night. I didn't like the idea but later on

I felt that the idea was after all not that bad. It makes the third day more thrilling and exciting.

On the third day for the "Bed of Flowers" ceremony the bed where we would sleep was decorated with flowers.

We were taken to the main hall on the 2nd floor where a second round of blessings was given to us. This time however by my relatives. It continued till about 2 PM.

The whole house was decorated earlier with lights and things. On that day the house was further decorated with fresh flowers, specially the rooms and the stairwell and the bedroom where we would spend our night. The walls were decorated with flower and garlands. The bed itself was covered with rose petals. The whole house was filled with sweet subtle fragrance of flowers. But at the rooftop, which was then covered, you would get only the strong smell of curry and Indian sweets. Almost 200 guests were invited for the dinner. At around 7:00 pm in the evening the invitees started coming in. I never realised that I had so many relatives and family friends in this city.

My wife sat on a throne-like-chair decorated with fresh flowers and peacock feathers. It was her day. Everyone wanted to see the bride and give their blessings and good wishes. On that day she was really looking very charming. Why not, she spent 2 hours on hairstyle, one hour on make-up and another one hour on dress and I was not allowed to come near her.

By around 12:00 at night all invitees had had their dinner and left after showering us with their good wishes and blessings. We were all extremely tired after this function and slept like logs as soon as our heads touched the pillow.

"Bed of Flowers" – where a new husband and his new wife are so tired that all they do is sleep.

9

LIFE IN INDIA

I had only three more days after the marriage, then I had to fly to Delhi to join the office. We could not make a programme for the honeymoon. These three days my wife and I just roamed around Kolkata city, its lakes and the gardens, both of us very new to each other, discovering each other. After three days I went to Delhi alone since I had to arrange for accommodation for my wife and I. I rented a two room flat in a suburb, which was about 5 kilometres away from my office. The flat or apartment was on the top floor of a three storied building. My mother and Mala came to Delhi after about 15 days. Life was good. My mother went back to Calcutta after about 2 months.

But one day I had a stroke of very bad luck. I had to stay out late at night to attend a trial of some wireless equipment. This was in the Defence Wireless Station to try out the night frequency. So I came back home at around 2:00 AM early morning. I parked my Scooter in the parking slot of the house. Went up to the second floor, then I realised that I had not taken the key to the apartment. I started banging on the door quite hard and loud. But the bedrooms were a bit away from the entrance door. I peeped out through the stair well window and saw the rain water drainpipe which was within the reach. If I could catch the drainpipe then I would be able to climb up and get down on the terrace of our flat. So I somehow pushed myself through the small stairwell window and caught hold of the drainpipe. When I started to climb the drainpipe I heard a very loud high pitch Police whistle. I looked down and saw with my horror, a Policeman waving a torch towards me. He was on his usual round during the night. I felt good to think that I was not the only one who had night duty. He shouted at me and asked me to climb down immediately. It was not an easy task, at least for me, to climb down the drainpipe from second floor to the ground level. As soon as I stepped on the ground the Policeman caught my hand and said,

"You burglar, house breaker! Come to the Police Station with me."

I had to shout back, "You shut up! What do you think who I am? Do I look like a burglar, a house breaker or a thief?"

Then I had to narrate to him what had happened. Our conversation was quite loud because we were almost shouting at each other. The Landlord who was living on the ground floor came out hearing our shouting. I think the Policeman and the Landlord knew each other. He then told the policeman that I was actually the tenant living in the top floor. The Policeman then gave me a big smile showing all his 32 teeth. I did not say a single word. I took the duplicate key from the Landlord and went to my apartment to sleep.

After a month or so I was temporarily transferred for 4 weeks to Bangalore which was about 1500 Kilometre south of Delhi. I was terribly annoyed when I got the news of my transfer. Next morning I went to the Managing Director's room. The Chief Executive Officer, who was my immediate boss, was also there. Both of them were Germans and were perfect gentlemen.

I said, "I have got a temporary transfer to Bangalore for 4 weeks. I was not allowed to take 2 weeks leave for my marriage. Three days after my marriage I had to come alone to Delhi. Now my wife is here and I had to do night duties. We were planning for a late honeymoon and now you are transferring me to Bangalore. If you don't want me to work here I am agreeable to resign".

Both of them started laughing and then the MD said, "Who told you that we do not want you to work with us? You have got a very good record and the Chief Executive Officer praises you very much. We definitely want you. You will have a very responsible job there. So about your private life, take your wife to Bangalore and enjoy your stay there."

I told, "It is easily said than done. You expect me to fly to Bangalore and stay in a Five Star Hotel for 4 weeks. I cannot afford that. This is simply beyond my means and you know that very well."

The Chief Executive Officer then told me, "Look Mr. Sarkar, all the extra expenses including your wife's air ticket will be on the house. Have your 4 weeks honeymoon in Bangalore. But do the job at the same time. I know you will be able to do that."

At first I could not believe what I heard. For few moments I could not speak anything, then I enquired, "Are you joking or…".

"No" he said, "We are serious".

I thanked them. That day I could not concentrate on my work properly. I was looking at my wristwatch the entire time. Then I could not wait further. With the permission of my boss I left the office an hour earlier than normal to give my wife the good news.

We went to Bangalore. It was a garden city. I would say it is a garden city but it is not so any more. It is now a city of concrete, better known as Silicon City in India within the industrial circle. We thoroughly enjoyed our stay in Bangalore. There were lots of good restaurants and many beautiful gardens. I was very happy with my work too. We came back to Delhi after about two months or so.

When Mala was expecting a baby, I was asked to go to Munich, West Germany, for a period of approximately six months. The Government factory in Bangalore, India, would manufacture our equipment and also the Mobile Radio Station. To finalise the design of the station which I had prepared and for the procurement process I was required to go to Germany. I wished Mala could also go with me. But we calculated that the baby would be very close to delivery when my work in Munich ended. Besides Mala would not be that much mobile during that time and because of that my work there might be hampered. It was better that she stayed back. It was a tough decision that I had to make to leave my wife and unborn child behind.

It was April 1965. We packed and sent everything to a store of a Furniture Removal Company. We flew to Calcutta first so that Mala could stay with her parents during my absence. After 2 days I flew to Munich. The work was going all right but my mind and my heart was always in Calcutta. The baby was due in the month of August. Work soon took over all my time and it flew by. I also had my old friends who were happy to give me company. Gerhard, Erika and Petra were very happy to see me again in Munich. I used to spend most of my weekends with them. I also made some new friends. Hence time was passing quite fast.

On 5th August in the afternoon I got the news which I was waiting for so eagerly. Mala had given birth to a baby girl. I had become a father. The news was so thrilling that I didn't know what to do or how to react. My entire being was filled with indescribable happiness and awe. I had never experienced such feelings before. I informed all my friends and Gerhard about this. I called some friends and spent the evening at a restaurant celebrating the birth of my daughter. By the end of August the Managing Director of Siemens in India came to Munich and said to me that I am to be transferred to Bangalore because the manufacturing of the equipment would be by Bharat Electronics Limited (BEL), a manufacturing company which is under the Ministry of Defence and would be co-ordinated from our Bangalore Office. Therefore instead of going back to Delhi I should go to Bangalore. I told him about my daughter and requested him for a week's holiday, which I would like to spend in Calcutta.

I returned to Calcutta by the end of September. By then my daughter, Arpita who is also called Nupur, was almost 2 months old. She looked exactly like me. Those who had seen her said that she was a carbon copy of me but miniature in size. A week flew by and the day came when I had to leave Calcutta. I left Calcutta alone for Bangalore feeling somewhat forlorn that I had to leave my loved ones behind but knew that they would soon be joining me.

This time I rented a 3-bedroom house. I arranged for the transportation of my furniture and all other household goods from Delhi to Bangalore. We slowly settled down. In my job I had to travel a lot within India. At least 15 days in a month I was out of Bangalore, but I used to enjoy my work.

The mobile wireless stations were being manufactured by Bharat Electronics Ltd, Bangalore, a central Government undertaking. Many of these wireless stations were extensively used during the war in the area then known as East Pakistan. After that war in 1971 East Pakistan became independent and Bangladesh, a free country, was born.

After a year, in October 1966, my wife gave birth to a baby boy. So our family grew from a single myself to the two of us and finally to us 4. I sold the scooter, which I had in Delhi after I had had an accident. I bought a car so that all of us could travel easily. In 1971 I had to go to Germany again. This time too Mala could not go with me because the children were too small and I was going again for only two months. I would be too busy with my work and would not be able to spend time on sight seeing.

In 1972 February I was transferred to our Electronics factory in Bombay as a Technical Manager. Again we had to pack up everything and then settle in Bombay. It was too difficult to get a reasonably good accommodation near the factory. Ultimately I found a good apartment house at a place called Santa Cruz West. I sold my Fiat 1100 car and bought an Indian made car, Ambassador Mark II, which was a bigger car and much more roomy and comfortable. The children got admitted to their schools. Everything was fine there and life was running smoothly. <<<<<<<<

In 1977 I again went to Germany for six months. This time I decided to take my wife with me to Europe. I negotiated with the company it was agreed that she would accompany me. Before we left for Europe my wife's parents came to Bombay to look after our children during our trip to Europe. We lived at many places in Europe, mostly in Germany. When we were in Munich we visited Gerhard's family. In fact we stayed in their house for two days. We enjoyed our stay in Europe very much. Mala liked Paris because of the Museums, Art Galleries and the architectural beauty of the old buildings. She loved Venice and London too. We stayed in Europe for about 7 months and came back to Bombay in October.

In the beginning of 1981 my sister and brother-in-law, who were living in Australia at that time, came to Bombay to visit us. One day when my brother-in-law and I were discussing about my work here, I told him that I had reached the top of my career ladder and any further move upwards was not possible.

He said, "So, if that is the case then why don't you come over to Australia. You have reached the top and you have already enjoyed your life there. Now try something else. Life in Australia is good and it will be definitely better than the life style you have here in Bombay."

I doubted it because I had lived in Europe and I doubted that it could be better than life in European countries.

I asked, "Am I not a bit old for migrating to another country? I am already 47 years of age."

He said, "Yes, just at the borderline. But you are an Engineer and have vast experience; it should not be a problem. If you decide to migrate to Australia then apply for it soon."

After a week or so they went back to Sydney. The idea of going to Australia was not bad but I was not completely confident. My daughter and son both were then studying in Year 10 – an important phase of their education. Would it be advisable to go to Australia at that time? After discussing it over and over with Mala and the children and spending few sleepless nights we decided to migrate. I then applied to the Australian Consulate for Permanent Residence Visas for all of us. I was really worried about migrating to Australia. It is easier to plant a sapling than to remove a fully-grown tree and put it at another place. I then consulted my boss at work about my migration to Australia and asked whether it would be possible to get an International Transfer from the Indian office to Australia to a comparable position. He advised me to apply and I did. And I also applied to Australian Head Office in Melbourne. After about two months or so and some correspondence, the personnel officer from the Melbourne office replied that it would be alright for them and the placement will be discussed when I arrive in Australia.

10

MIGRATING TO AUSTRALIA

We landed in Sydney on 22 June 1982. My brother-in-law came to the Airport to receive us. My sister had two daughters. The younger one was studying in New South Wales University and was living with them. The elder one was married and had a son of 2 years old at that time and was living in Calcutta. But they all came to Sydney on a long holiday. We decided to stay with my sister in Sydney for a few days and then go to Melbourne to take up my job.

On 24th June I took the early morning bus from Sydney and reached Melbourne on the same day evening. It was quite dark when we reached the Interstate Bus Terminal in Melbourne. I had only a small carry bag with me. My brother-in-law talked to one of his friends in Melbourne and told him that I would stay only for a day or two with them. Since I did not know the place I took a Taxi and gave the address to the driver. Their house was not far from the bus terminal. I was feeling little bit embarrassed because I had never met them earlier and after all they are known to my brother-in-law and not to me. I pressed the doorbell. Mr Day, friend of my brother-in-law, opened the door and asked me who I was. I introduced myself and told that I was sorry I could not phone him before I left Sydney. He told, "Don't worry, your sister rang up this morning and told us about you.

We then talked about an hour or so and then went for the dinner. The night was very cold. I was very tired due to the long bus journey from Sydney to Melbourne. I expressed my desire to go to bed early. Mrs Day then showed me the room where I would stay. The room was very cold. I requested for a room heater. I slept like a log.

Next day in the morning I rang up the company where I was supposed to take up my job. I came to Melbourne to discuss with the Personnel Department. When I rang up The Personnel Manager was surprised that I was already in Melbourne.

I reached the office at around 10 O'clock for the meeting. I was told by the Personnel Manager that the Managing Director was in Germany. The company was running in red and therefore nothing could be done now. I would have to wait for the Managing Director and he was expected to come back after 2 months. In fact they were offering redundancy packages to their employees.

That year, 1982, was very bad for employment and Australia had been hit with a deep recession. The percentage of unemployment was very high. I felt upset with the turn of events. They should have written to me in detail about the situation prevailing at that time. Instead the Personnel Manager wrote me that it would be all right for them if I came to Australia and the placement would be discussed when I arrived in Australia. In fact he sent me a letter to my office address in India explaining the financial condition of the company and the high unemployment rate in Australia at that time. In that letter he advised me to postpone my coming to Australia. But I missed that letter as I took 3 months off between my resignation from Siemens India and joining Siemens Australia. During those 3 months we (my whole family) went on holidays to Cashmere and Goa. Before we left for Australia we spend few days in Calcutta. I do not blame Melbourne office. The whole thing had just misfired.

I left Melbourne on the same day by catching a night bus. I reached Sydney next morning. I explained everything to my family. They were all very upset. I did not have any job and how long could four extra people stay with my sister? We were eight adults living there in a three-bedroom apartment house. In the meantime we became acquainted with some families of the Bengali community.

One day we were invited by one of my sister's friends for dinner. There I was asked by someone to apply for the unemployment dole. I felt ashamed of the very idea of unemployment dole. But then it was explained to me that we had migrated to Australia and I would be working here till I retire. I would be paying income tax for my earning. There is nothing bad in it to accept unemployment dole because I would be paying back to the Government by way of taxes much more than what I would take as dole and then again it would be for few weeks only. So I applied for the unemployment dole and started getting it after two weeks or so.

I started applying for jobs at various places. In the meantime I was trying for alternative accommodation. Ultimately we managed to get a 3-room accommodation in the Migrants Hostel which was not very far from my sister's place. The Hostel was reasonably good. It had a very big communal dining room and a big kitchen where foods were prepared for the people staying in the Hostel. It had a big common room where at least 50 people could sit and watch TV programmes. The TV was set to one channel and no one supposed to change the channel without the permission of the warden. During that time the Cricket World Cup started. My son was a stern fan of cricket. But the hostel guests were not interested to watch cricket, rather they preferred to watch M*A*S*H and other regular programmes. I hated to see the sad look on my son's face. I did not have enough money to buy a TV. I took some loan and bought a TV of a very basic model. The happiness I saw in my children was worth more than the money I spent on the TV. They could watch the Cricket World cup sitting in their room.

Within 3 months I got an offer for two jobs. One from Canberra and the other was from Sydney. Though the Canberra job was better I chose to stay in Sydney. My daughter and the son were already admitted to schools and we had started liking Sydney.

I joined a N.S.W. State Public Service and had to start from a lower level. Slowly I again climbed the ladder of success. After a few years of service I reached a level where I was happy and secure. To achieve this we all had to struggle quite a lot -especially Mala who had had a very leisurely and comfortable life since she had been born. Whatever we have achieved today is no doubt due to her hard work.

Our daughter and son have married, have their own families and are happily settled in Sydney. My son is also an engineer like myself and graduated from the University of New South Wales.

We have frequent family get together with dinners, BBQs, anniversaries, birthdays and life is happy and full.

I recall what my brother-in-law once said when he visited us in Bombay during 1981. He said my life style would not be bad in Australia, rather it would be better. He was right in a way since my migration has proved to be good for my children's future and their education.

Mala and I wanted to go back to India after my retirement. We have a very strong bond with India. All our relatives are there. We have been born and brought up in India. Blood ties cannot be forgotten so easily. But we will not be able to go back to our original home country forever. Our children are here. Our grandchildren are here. They have more or less adopted the Australian life style. We the first generation always suffer. We cannot go back since our near and dear ones are in Australia and pull us back. But we also feel restless here since India has permeated in our blood. The only solution would be to stay here for half the year and stay in India for the other half as long as health permits. When either of us become partially immobile and cannot travel anymore we will remain close to where our children are.

I have thus seen all the beautiful colours of my life. Now at the fag end of my life I am just waiting to see how this Rainbow slowly fades away and vanishes leaving behind only a few memories.